"In *TeamMakers*, Laura Robb and Evan Robb offer educators a passion-fueled 'dream template.' Inspired by seventy-nine varied forms of the word "dream" scattered across the book, we are asked to shift our view from what is to what could be. Laura and Evan show us how to break free of excuses that obstruct our view so that we can bravely envision the possibilities awaiting us at the edge of uncertainty. Encouraging examples of empowered educators and students provide the vision for repositioning children squarely at the center of our efforts. *TeamMakers* is an invitational *how to* for translating professional dreams into transformational actions."

—Dr. Mary Howard, author of *Good to Great Teaching*

"Laura Robb and Evan Robb combine their experiences, their talents, and their passions for the schools children deserve to bring us a rich and accessible resource. In this book, readers are encouraged to push past what has been, to reach beyond what is, and to dream. Laura and Evan invite us to risk imagining what could be, to envision and work together to build strong and honest relationships with our students and our colleagues that enable us to pull our feet from the muck of tradition and march forward toward our professional vision. The text moves gently between the voices of Laura and Evan with the voices of students, administrators, and teachers woven into this exquisite fabric devoted to authentic teaching and learning."

—Lester Laminack, coauthor of *Reading to Make a Difference*

"Laura and Evan have crafted a beautiful professional text, one that is filled with practical advice and sound thinking for teachers and administrators. They show, through story, the power of dreams, the magnitude of relationships, and the importance of conversations among stakeholders in education. This book is full of hope and passion, and with each passing chapter, the need for change builds into a lovely crescendo, nudging us to change the way we think about our schools and ultimately our students. I urge you to read this book. It caused me to fall in love with teaching all over again. And I know it will do the same for you."

—S. Travis Crowder, coauthor of *Sparks in the Dark*

"*TeamMakers* is filled with practical ideas for empowering teachers, leaders, and learners. We must reinvent education to meet the demands of the future. We can't prepare students for a rapidly changing world with a status quo education. Laura and Evan have created a wonderful blueprint for creating relevant, dynamic learning with today's students in mind. Our schools can be places of greater meaning, purpose, and hope."

—**David Guerin**, author of *Future Driven*

"Laura and Evan Robb are both incredible and inspiring educators and leaders in the field. Throughout *TeamMakers*, I was reminded of just how lucky I was to be learning alongside of them through their words on the page. Practical ideas, honesty, and heart flow through this book. I felt like I was spending time with old friends all while walking away with new ideas and a renewed sense of passion. This book should be in the hands of every educator."

—**Todd Nesloney**, author of *Stories from WEBB*

"What a delightful read! Too many education books get bogged down in research and statistics, and the beauty of this collection of stories is it reminds educators why we do what we do for a living—prepare students for their future. This book is a must for schools interested in building collaborative teams that are dedicated to having reflective conversations of what works best for students."

—**Danny Brassell**, author of *Bring Joy Back into the Classroom*

"Stories are the heart of a society and Laura and Evan Robb, along with their collaborators, are master storytellers who share their informative lessons of leadership and learning. Aptly titled *TeamMakers: Positively Impacting Students through District-Wide Dreaming, Collaborating and Change* this book uses stories to guide leaders to create schools that are truly learning centered for preparing students for a rapidly changing world. They weave together a range of voices and perspectives to help guide leaders and learners in districts that may vary greatly but face the same key issues around planning and collaboration. Throughout the seventeen chapters are voices from the field in the Interludes that extend the story with practical real world examples. And each chapter ends with Reflect! Discuss with Colleagues! Revisit! Share! That's just what readers will want to do as they read this book."

—**Adria Klein**, coauthor of *SMALL-GROUP Reading Instruction*

TeamMakers

Positively Impacting the Lives of Children through District-Wide

Dreaming, Collaborating, and Change

ra Robb   Evan Robb

TEAMMAKERS

© 2019 by Laura Robb and Evan Robb

This book is available at special discounts when purchased in quantity for use as premiums, promotions, fundraisers, or for educational use. For inquiries and details, contact the publisher at books@daveburgessconsulting.com.

Published by Dave Burgess Consulting, Inc.
San Diego, CA
http://daveburgessconsulting.com

Cover Design by Genesis Kohler
Editing and Interior Design by My Writers' Connection

Library of Congress Control Number: 2019944126
Paperback ISBN: 978-1-949595-54-3
Ebook ISBN: 978-1-949595-55-0
First Printing: July 2019

DEDICATION

With deep thanks to all the administrators, teachers, and students we have learned from and who have become the beacons lighting our educational journey.

 —Laura Robb and Evan Robb

CONTENTS

DEAR EDUCATORS,

Neither of us ever envisioned ourselves as educators, but circumstances sent us down unexpected paths. Evan has now served as a principal for more than twenty years. Laura has invested more than forty-five years in teaching grades four through eight and now works closely with Evan as a literacy coach and consultant. Together we have explored the experiences, leadership, and relationships necessary for building a strong, positive school community. Those stories and experiences are what led us to write this book.

In college I (Laura) majored in English and French literature. After graduation, I wrote copy for an advertising agency in New York City. In 1963, my husband, Lloyd, took a job teaching voice at Shenandoah University in Winchester, Virginia, a small city with no ad agencies. I was in a strange city and state where I knew no one. I desperately needed a job. Armed with a provisional teaching certificate, I applied for a sixth-grade position in a country school and discovered my passion: teaching.

I (Evan) never intended to teach either. After receiving my MBA, I searched for a job in business but, because of the weak economy at the time, few jobs were available in Winchester or in the surrounding area. To stay busy and earn some money, I applied to substitute teach in Clarke County and Winchester City Public Schools. I quickly discovered that kindergarten and first grade were not for me, but I felt deeply connected to teaching and learning with middle school students and applied to several districts for a full-time position. In 1992, I began teaching history to seventh graders and, like Mom, I fell in love with teaching and knew education would be my lifelong profession.

Recently, when Mom and I have shared teaching stories, our focus has been on the need for school districts to morph into learning centers preparing students for a future with many unknowns. We have a dream for school districts—a vision we'd love to see become a reality! We're hoping for great teamwork and collaborations among the superintendents, their assistants, school principals, other school leaders, and teachers on district-wide initiatives affecting all schools: student-centered learning, best practice instruction, differentiation, personalization of learning, using technology integration to enhance learning, creating a district-wide culture of reading, and using formative assessment.

Predicting what technology and the world in general will be like in ten, fifteen, or twenty years is impossible, and this realization pushed us to dream about and reflect on how schools can better prepare students for this uncertainty. Mom and I started dreaming separately, then shared our individual visions, and ultimately began imagining together. The result has been an avalanche of ideas.

We arranged selected shared dreams under the microscope of our imaginations, played with them through conversations, and focused on the skills students would need to wrestle with their future unknowns. We agreed that the ability to collaborate, imagine what no one else imagined, analyze information, and problem solve would help students cope with seemingly insurmountable challenges. In the following chapters, we have laid out our shared dreams and vision for how school district personnel—superintendents, principals, teachers, as well as all administrative and support staff—can come together to evolve schools into learning centers better able to equip students with these skills.

We also invited some central office and school administrators, teachers, and students to share personal experiences in short pieces we call interludes. Their visions and voices expand on our thoughts and offer unique insight into specific topics throughout the book. The three high school students from northern Virginia, Leila Mohajer, Joe O'Such, and Sam Fremin, are members of #BOWTIE, a group of middle and high school students who work with high school English teacher, Jason Augustowski. #BOWTIE conduct educational research from within the trenches and mix this experience with reading the most influential professional education books of the day. At school, they work alongside teachers to build a learning community that offers students voice and choice.

Each chapter closes with questions for personal reflection and discussion with colleagues. Additionally, at the end of the first and last parts of the book, we've included a QR code for a short podcast we have created.

Dreams and stories are the sum of who we are. We invite you to use your creativity and imagination to reach further than your grasp and encourage teamwork and meaningful communication among schools and the central office. We invite you to be TeamMakers who will dream and story with us to reimagine leadership, teaching, curriculum, and learning.

—Laura Robb and Evan Robb

PART I
Looking Backward to Move Forward

When Evan and I think of change, teamwork enters our minds. We call this book *TeamMakers* because we believe that when the central office staff and entire school community intentionally collaborate and communicate, their ability to create positive change in teaching and learning far outweighs a neatly written plan. The opening three chapters lay the foundation for teamwork and change.

Both of us want students to experience learning that's real but also sustained and nourished with hopes and dreams. My story of learning to play the piano with a cardboard keyboard has a lot to say about the kinds of learning experiences some schools offer students. Such experiences might start with the best of intentions, but sometimes they just don't work.

The changes in teaching and learning we seek can occur if district-wide teams share their stories, dreams, and beliefs and use these to build relationships and connect with their creativity and ability to analyze—some of the skills students will need for their futures. Making these connections can support making shifts in beliefs about teaching and learning based on personal experiences.

Evan and I invite you to read and reflect on the stories we share and move to a place where you boldly shift your thinking and develop the growth mindset needed to become a TeamMaker and team member! We also ask you to get in touch with your stories and use them to shape your beliefs about teaching, learning, and effective change.

Instead of "pockets of change" in a school district, Evan and I hope *TeamMakers* can provide you with the tools to make significant and sustainable changes in all schools. Communicate and collaborate to empower yourself and others to dream high, reach for the stars, and create schools that become learning centers preparing students to be the creative problem solvers the world needs.

CHAPTER 1
DREAMS AND STORIES

———

When I (Laura) was in the sixth grade in a public school in The Bronx, New York, group piano lessons were offered to the students. I begged my mom to sign the permission form allowing me to participate, and she did. In fact, I can still hear her telling my father, "Poor children can take piano lessons! What a great idea."

Before entering the auditorium for the first lesson, every aspiring pianist received a cardboard keyboard for practicing and playing simple pieces. Miss Gilder, the teacher, stood on the stage along with a real piano and her own giant cardboard keyboard, as incapable of making sound as our smaller versions. She played a short piece on the piano and then banged it out on the enormous keyboard. Next it was our turn. My heart fell when we tried it on our keyboards. I couldn't hear any music. I could only hear the thumps of fingers pounding on cardboard keyboards. By the end of the second week, the one hundred hopeful pianists had dwindled to ten. Before long there were none.

In more than forty-five years of teaching, I've seen initiatives like the group piano lessons and speed reading come and go. And consider all the changes in technology. Popular at one time, but gone now, were film loops and film strip machines, television sets in kindergarten to eighth grade classrooms for watching educational programming, and cassette players for listening to authors, stories, and music. All of these seemed so cutting edge at one time, but Evan and I chuckle when we think about them today.

Some things about education have not changed. I (Evan) frequently point out to teachers and administrators that my grandfather would feel right at home in many secondary schools today, and he immigrated to the United States from Poland when he was sixteen—in 1922! Students still sit in rows, copy notes from the chalkboard, and listen to the teacher lecture from a desk or from the front of the room just as they did when he was in school. Changes in education aren't keeping up with advances in technology, how information is accessed, how students learn, and how the Internet has created a global learning community through Twitter, Facebook, and email. While administrators equip classrooms with white boards, computers, and tablets, in many classrooms, technology is simply an ornament. How students learn hasn't changed. Look carefully at what students do and how teachers organize learning on tablets and computers. Technology can be deceptive. Because learning can still mirror practices popular in the nineteenth century, how can schools ensure they are moving students into the twenty-first century?

Part of the answer is through continually changing technology, instructional materials, and books. However, the real key lies with education's North Star: educators and their capacity to dream and imagine. People are vital to a school's success! No program or scripted curriculum can replace highly skilled, compassionate teachers who monitor students' progress, provide academic support, and nurture an "I can learn" spirit.

All schools deserve principals who forge trusting relationships, extend kindness to everyone, lead in instruction, participate in professional learning with staff, and know and care about every student. Sharing dreams and stories is an important way to build these relationships. Moreover, when staff and administrators share with students dreams and personal stories about their teaching and learning lives, students feel safe to share theirs. Sharing dreams and stories builds positive relationships. In turn these relationships build trust, create strong bonds, and have the power to change students' and adults' narratives.

THE STUFF OF DREAMS

One of the most frequently used words in the plays and sonnets of Shakespeare is *dream*. The wizard Prospero in *The Tempest* forges deep connections between dreams and stories when he says, "We are such stuff as dreams are made on, and our little life is rounded with sleep." Yes! Dreams of your hopes, who you want to become, and where you desire to travel are all imagined stories. Some become real; others continue to dwell deep in your memory waiting for a problem, obstacle, or goal to resurrect them. Story dreams are part of who you are. They are personal revelations and have the power to change narratives and alter thinking and actions.

I (Laura) watched such a transformation this past school year when I worked every day with a group of fifth graders who started the school year reading at an early first-grade level. For two months, when I pointed out progress they were making in reading, they shook their heads "no" and mumbled, "We can't learn reading." I wondered why they couldn't see or accept the improvement I observed. I took a different tack. Once a week, I shared one of my dreams and then asked them to share one of theirs. They looked at me as if I had metamorphosed into an alien visiting earth from a remote planet. My request was always met with silence and eyes staring down at the table.

DREAMING TRANSFORMS THE ORDINARY INTO THE EXTRAORDINARY.

This exchange continued until a month later, when Rosa looked up and whispered, "I want to be a vet. I love animals." Immediately, Rosa's narrative began to change. "I have to learn reading to be a vet," she said. For the rest of the year, Rosa selected books every day to read at home, something she had refused to do before this magical moment. Her reading skill improved because her dream linked her to the importance of practicing reading. After the group finished reading *Stone Fox* by John Reynolds Gardiner, Rosa declared, "I am a reader!" A few days later, three more students shared their dreams. Ricardo wanted to be a computer whiz, Omar dreamed of becoming a scientist who studies monkeys, and Maria aspired to be a law enforcement officer.

I believe dreams empowered these students to open their hearts and minds to see and accept that they were becoming readers. Their dreams unstuck their stories and transformed them into hopeful, dedicated, and hardworking students who eventually acknowledged their improvement in reading skill that I had observed every day.

DREAMING AND STORYTELLING
TO EFFECT CHANGE

Dreaming is so much more than brainstorming. It's an invitation to stretch your imagination, be daring, let go, and embrace the stories of possibilities—even those seemingly irrelevant and impossible to achieve. Dreaming transforms the ordinary into the extraordinary. Dreaming makes an artist of the dreamer, offering a rich palette of possibilities and a myriad of choices.

We believe dreams and stories must play a role in schools making the leap from nineteenth century teaching and learning practices to experiences students need to become problem solvers and creative thinkers. We encourage schools to set aside time for dreaming so staff and administrators can use their storytelling minds to meet challenges with imagination and creativity. We also encourage school administrators and staff to share their stories and dreams. Make dreaming, getting in touch with your stories, and sharing them part of your mission. Be passionate about creating stories to effect change—change to help children want to learn, love reading, and reach for their own dreams. As you chart your dreaming journey, remember your primary goal is to focus on the students who depend on you to prepare them for their tomorrows.

REFLECT! **DISCUSS WITH COLLEAGUES!** **REVISIT!**

- How have dreams and stories affected your life and beliefs? How have they affected the lives of your students?
- How can you find more time to share, discuss, and act on your dreams?

—— **Share your thoughts and ideas! #teammakers** ——

CHAPTER 2
SHIFTING TO EFFECTIVELY PREPARING STUDENTS

The United States Department of Education states that the mission of public education is to ". . . promote student achievement and preparation for global competitiveness by fostering educational excellence and ensuring equal access." We wholeheartedly support this simply stated mission! It alludes to changes schools can adopt to ensure students are ready for their futures in a world connected by technology, science, trade, education, arts, and business. But what are these shifts and how can our schools make them?

As we reflected on the mission statement, we agreed there were several ways teachers can "promote student achievement." Providing authentic reading and writing experiences with self-selected books and writing topics, encouraging students to write original responses to texts, and inviting students to discuss their reading with a partner or in a small group all foster student achievement. If teachers question what makes learning authentic, we encourage them to ask, "Do I do it? Would I do it?" If the answer is, "no!" then don't ask kids to do it.

READY FOR CHANGE

A few years ago, I (Laura) conducted a survey among eighth graders in a local middle school, asking, "What kinds of learning experiences do you value? Explain why." I conducted this survey after observing the classes of three English teachers the principal hired me to coach. The similarities between the classes were startling: students sat in rows, completed worksheets, exchanged papers, scored them, and turned them in to the teachers. Students read the same book and completed thick packets of pre-made worksheets. All the responses I received to the survey were similar to these:

- I hate worksheets. They're boring. In social studies, we work in groups. Each group gets a topic, and we read and discuss. We share with the class. I like that.
- I can't even read the book, so how can I do the worksheets? I want to choose my books.
- We never talk. Just do worksheets. Same thing every day. Boring!

Not one student out of the three classes declared a love of worksheets and novel packets, and none of them enjoyed slogging through books they couldn't comprehend. Moreover, worksheets and packets send two negative messages to students: First, they communicate that teachers choose books and materials because they don't trust student choices. Second, they say teachers don't value student ideas about texts and their ability to express them during discussions and conferences or write about them in a reader's notebook.

Teachers shared their dissatisfaction with the poor and incomplete work students did and complained about students who turned in blank worksheets because they couldn't read the book. Of course students did this. Expecting them to learn from and answer questions about materials they can't understand is unreasonable. Over time this results in diminishing students' self-confidence, risk-taking, and desire to improve.

Almost as frustrated as their students, the teachers seemed ready for change. I shared the students' survey responses, hoping they would rattle teachers' beliefs and set the stage for reading professional materials and dreaming. Sometimes, as the teachers read the responses, flashes of anger swept across their faces. To their credit, the teachers stepped beyond hurt feelings and blaming students. Knowing how difficult change can be, I promised to support them and give them the time needed to learn, dream of changes, reflect, and grow. When the principal purchased six hundred books for each classroom library, the teachers turned the corner of doubt, recognizing that he supported instructional changes, and our journey to replace teacher-centered narratives with student-centered stories began.

CHANGE TAKES TIME

All shifts gain depth and staying power when the journey is slow and steady. The poet, Eve Merriam's words, "It takes a lot of slow to grow," are true for adults and children and can steer a school's course when it's reflecting on "global competitiveness by fostering educational excellence."

Global competitiveness depends on a country's ability to advance educational excellence and prepare generations for their future. For students to compete nationally and internationally, schools' curricula, teaching, and learning practices should provide opportunities for creative and critical thinking, problem-solving, and teamwork. Schools have a responsibility to send students into the workforce or to college with the skills they need to be successful.

I RESISTED SETTING TIME FRAMES FOR IMPLEMENTING CHANGES. TEACHERS TOOK THE PLUNGE WHEN THEY FELT READY.

As principal of Johnson Williams Middle School, I (Evan) continually engage with staff to integrate collaboration, communication, creativity, critical thinking, and choice into our curriculum. However, it took time for all teachers to feel comfortable and capable in this model. When I initiated this, I expected fast-track change among teachers. But Merriam's words reverberated in my mind. Even after they read and discussed professional articles, teachers asked for extra time to absorb the information and observe student-centered classes in other schools. They also needed to experience integrating specific skills into lessons.

At this point, I changed the content and focus of our faculty, team, and department meetings. At least twice a month, teachers read, discussed, and analyzed a professional article. They worked in teams to choose ideas from their discussions and transfer them into their teaching. They shared lessons, explaining what worked, and asking for feedback on what needed improvement. By actively doing, teachers experienced student-centered learning.

Although it was sometimes tough for me, I resisted setting time frames for implementing changes. Teachers took the plunge when they felt ready. I supported teachers as they shared lessons, asking their colleagues to point out what did and didn't work as well. This showed them I valued their taking risks and trusted their judgment. I sent emails and notes to teachers who shared lessons at meetings and celebrated their growth and integration of skills necessary for student success. I never criticized if they tried and weren't successful. I built on what worked. I gave teachers professional learning opportunities, choice, and the gift of time.

As teachers became more comfortable and slowly moved to student-centered learning, we were then able to discuss and decide on changes in curriculum. For example, to better prepare students for college or a career after high school, we added a year-long technology elective for students in sixth through eighth grades to learn web design, coding, and app creation. STEM (science, technology, engineering, and mathematics) has become a focus of our school because staff and I know that many future jobs will include technology, science, math, and engineering. By reflecting on and updating curriculum, schools can offer students equal access to classes that will directly impact their future.

CHANGING THE CULTURE

When teachers and administrators feel they've arrived at their final educational station and have nothing more to learn, curiosity wanes, dreams die, and growth stops. However, an educational journey should never end, because students, families, and communities change. New research, professional articles, and current books are available to inspire and raise questions about present beliefs. Because of this, we envision a continually evolving culture for school districts, especially in these cases:

- Stakeholders are free to dream and implement big ideas that can push schools beyond what they've always done to new places.

- Individual schools can choose school-wide initiatives.
- Professional learning for staff and administrators is a high priority.
- Technology connects all members of a school district through podcasts, videos, and school and district websites.

When members of a school district are informed and experiencing joy and pride in their school's daily events and annual initiatives, they build a strong, interconnected community. When they discover and nurture collective dreams, they can make positive and significant change. Simon Sinek said, "Dr. King gave the 'I Have a Dream' speech, not the 'I Have a Plan' speech." Plans are earthbound and ordinary and, while educators use them to reach objectives, they don't accomplish what dreaming does. Dreams are imaginary and celestial, and they push educators to connect with and advocate for every child they encounter.

REFLECT! DISCUSS WITH COLLEAGUES! REVISIT!

- What meaningful connections among all school district members act as a catalyst for change and prepare students for their future?
- What shifts can you make to impact positive change within your school or classroom?

—— **Share your thoughts and ideas! #teammakers** ——

CHAPTER 3
MINDSETS MADE FOR CHANGE

Evan's high school biology teacher, Mr. Wendell, nailed down his curriculum after his second year of teaching. Afterward, repetition characterized his lectures, lab demonstrations, unit study sheets, and grueling multiple choice and fill-in-the-blank tests. Teaching for Mr. Wendell equaled delivering the same curriculum year after year after year. Content was king! Responding to students' individual needs wasn't in his lexicon. Students were to copy notes, listen, remember, study, memorize facts, and do well on tests.

Fast-forward eighteen years. Evan's son, Bobby, is now taking biology, and Mr. Wendell is *his* teacher—and nothing has changed! He is using the same lectures, the same unit study guides, and the same tests. Uninterested in personal growth, building positive relationships with students, and improving and updating the content of instruction, Mr. Wendell is a prime example of a teacher with a fixed mindset who says things like:

- It was good enough for me, so it's good enough for my students.
- We've always done things this way; we don't need to change.
- *My curriculum is set; I'm not changing it.*

Educators need to remember they teach *children*, not scripted curricula or basal or computer programs. We encourage teachers to question rigid pacing guides requiring every student be in the same place on a specific day. Because the emotional and academic needs of children differ, we believe teachers are responsible for observing their students' learning. They actively listen during discussions and conferences, read written work, and then identify the lessons, support, and interventions children need to improve. When teachers do this, students are placed at the center of learning and experience greater success at school.

GROWTH MINDSET

Carol Dweck's book, *Mindset: The New Psychology of Success* (2007), discusses how a growth mindset influences leadership, thinking, actions, decision-making, dreaming, and reaching goals. As a principal, I (Evan) encourage staff and students to cultivate and nurture a growth mindset.

Although mindset choice may seem simple, it isn't; however, if you fully embrace a positive mindset, it can have a profound impact on you and those around you. Often, I meet with parents who tell me they could "never do math," and therefore their child can't do it. Unfortunately, this pattern of predicting what children can and cannot do can run through generations, diminishing their academic and career choices. Additionally, if a teacher's comments to a student reinforce the student's negative belief in his/her own ability to learn, they will adversely affect the student's self-image and mindset. On the other hand, if the child experiences a teacher who lives and communicates a growth mindset, that student will see that an opportunity for progress is always possible. For example, the next time a student says, "I can't do math," respond using growth mindset language such as, "You can't do math *yet*, but with support and hard work you *will* be able to do it."

Below are my top five growth mindset beliefs. Whether you're an administrator or teacher, when you live these daily, you can influence others to cultivate their own growth mindset.

1. **View problems and challenges as opportunities for change and growth.** They are part of life, work, and school. Seeing problems as unsolvable challenges or as opportunities to overcome, improve, and grow is a personal choice.

2. **Redefine "brilliant."** Too often people focus on the achievements of others instead of on the effort it takes to progress; they

assume others are "naturally brilliant." But most adults and students are not naturally brilliant. They work hard to reach their goals. They develop understanding and achievement through effort. Everyone learns new information or concepts in different ways and at different speeds; this reflects a growth mindset and leads to true brilliance.

3. **Make *learning* part of your vocabulary.** People with a growth mindset are always learning. Plus, the way you respond to people who say they can't learn something new can disrupt their fixed mindset and influence them ultimately to transform it into a growth mindset.

4. **Change your view of criticism.** Don't take criticism personally. When you resist emotional reactions to criticism, you can see it as an opportunity to grow, solve problems, and often collaborate.

5. **Use the word "yet."** Dweck says "not yet" has become one of her favorite phrases. If you haven't solved a problem yet, you can solve it with hard work and support later!

Self-efficacy and collective efficacy are kindred souls to growth mindset. Self-efficacy is believing you have the capacity and ability to do something you thought you couldn't do. It's an "I can do it" attitude mirroring a person's confidence and motivation toward school and life. It also can have a powerful trickle-down effect. When more and more people in a school district have strong self-efficacy, collective efficacy develops. In turn, the positive energy released by collective efficacy

SELF-EFFICACY AND COLLECTIVE EFFICACY ARE KINDRED SOULS TO GROWTH MINDSET.

can transform schools' problems and challenges into changes benefiting all stakeholders, especially children.

To maintain a growth mindset and self-efficacy, administrators and teachers benefit by carving out reflective time as well as time to relax and enjoy their families and do what they love! Marlena Gross-Taylor stresses the importance of taking time to renew and recharge your teaching and leadership energy.

TAKING A BREATH
An Interlude by Marlena Gross-Taylor

Educators endeavor to inspire. They want to inspire their students, fellow teachers, and, if they are in a leadership position, those who follow them. But have you ever considered the definition of the word inspire? It is translated from the Latin word *insperitae* meaning "to breathe." If educators are to *inspire* and encourage creativity in others, it's imperative they prioritize their own white space to recharge.

How do you carve out time for white space as an educator? Consider these four ways to take a breath:

1. **Reflection.** Consider your daily routines. When are you able to have a moment to yourself without any obligations? Maybe you have time in the car ride to and from school or even in those few moments before you start your day. Choose a time best for you and commit to reflecting on the present. Instead of mentally running through your ever-growing to-do list, this should be a time to reflect on what you're grateful for or what inspires you each day.

2. **Planning.** Just as you must be intentional with embedding your standards in your lesson plans, you must be just as vigilant in planning white space. A full calendar doesn't necessarily reflect productivity. Set aside time on your calendar to relax, daydream, and grab a cup of coffee with friends. If you're worried about those menial tasks consuming precious chunks of your time—like cleaning your house or bathing the dog—consider outsourcing those tasks to free up time for yourself.

3. **Family.** Educators' families often take the back seat to their students, school, and community. Early in my career, I had to live with the guilt of missing a few of my boys' milestones because I was teaching or leading. Set clear boundaries between work and family, and plan around important milestones even if it means taking time off to attend a field trip or sporting event.

4. **Passions.** I absolutely love being an educator and accept the full responsibility of impacting children's' lives. However, teaching

is not my only passion. I feel like Betty White in the Snickers commercial if I go too long without curling up in my favorite chair to read or tucking myself away in my office to write. What is your passion? Better yet, how do you make time to engage in your passion? Through your passions, you can deepen your connection with students.

White space provides clarity, allowing you to refocus on your purpose: to inspire the next generation and, hopefully, model the importance of taking a breath.

TAKE THE PULSE

We urge you to take the pulse of your school's culture, collective efficacy, and growth mindset by reflecting on the following questions.

- Are there disconnects between your school's mission statement and the mindsets of staff? If so, what steps can you take to repair them?
- Are there disconnects between what administrators and staff say and do? If so, how can reflection, dreaming, storytelling, and debriefing confront and change these?
- How does collective efficacy support growth and change among students and staff?
- How can administrators nurture a growth mindset and collective efficacy among staff and students?
- How can the superintendent and team help create collective efficacy and a growth mindset among all staff?

When all members of a school district have growth mindsets and collective efficacy, they have the people power to transform problems and challenges into opportunities for growth. Yes, mindsets matter! Dreams, a growth mindset, and collective efficacy fuel positive change and put children first, surrounding them with kindness, empathy, love, and the support needed to find their own dreams and greatness!

REFLECT! DISCUSS WITH COLLEAGUES! REVISIT!

- What do your dreams and stories tell about your mindset?
- Reflect on your schedule and consider ways you can find additional time for reflection, planning, family, and passions.

—— **Share your thoughts and ideas! #teammakers** ——

QR CODE FOR PODCAST
TEAMMAKERS, GETTING STARTED

PART II
Examining and Reimagining

In this section, Evan and I point out and discuss school practices such as extra credit and compliance that we hope will disappear, and we offer alternatives to discuss and embrace. The end goal is to develop teaching and learning practices that best serve the needs of students living in a world with dramatic technological advances and a global interconnectedness that is here to stay.

Evan and I redefine traditional roles of superintendent and assistant superintendent as well as building-level leadership. Here's where you'll be able to experience and feel the energy that being a TeamMaker can bring to your school district.

We envision a depth of communication among staff that is new to most schools. For all stakeholders in a district to drive their positive energy to a key purpose, we imagine the principal fostering and nurturing teacher and student leadership. The belief that we're stronger together affects central office and school administrators as well as teachers and staff in a district, often resulting in a commitment to personal growth and developing a common vision. The positive energy of such district-wide empowerment can create learning environments and curricula capable of transforming students into global citizens who can think critically and imagine what others believed was impossible!

CHAPTER 4
SCHOOL PRACTICES TO ELIMINATE

For school districts to effectively prepare students for the future, some schools' practices need to go! We laugh sometimes when we discuss these, because they send us back to our own experiences in elementary, middle, and high school. At other times, we feel disheartened, realizing such practices continue to thrive in many schools today.

I (Evan) remember facing one of these practices when I attended parents' night. My son, Bobby, started the fifth grade and was in a multiage class of fourth- and fifth-grade students. A "wall" of bookcases separated the grade levels, and each grade had its own blackboard, clearly marked at the top with *fourth graders* and *fifth graders*. Mr. Thompson, the teacher, explained to the parents that he alternated working with students: while he taught the fourth graders, the fifth-grade students completed worksheets, and vice versa. The grades never did anything together.

After Mr. Thompson reviewed his class rules and expectations, he asked parents whether they had questions. One question remains imprinted in my memory because everyone—except me—agreed it was important: *How can my child get extra credit?* Mr. Thompson proceeded to explain that our children could raise their test grades by bringing in a box of tissues, pencils, or notebook paper or by completing extra worksheets and following class rules to the "T."

Interestingly, the principal respected Mr. Thompson because he kept his students "in line." Compliance was expected. Noncompliant students might receive zeros on assignments, be required to sit in the desk labeled "for misbehaving students," or be assigned physical tasks such as washing desks, blackboards, clapping erasers, and writing "I will follow the rules" fifty to one hundred times. Parents applauded Mr. Thompson's strict discipline. They were also pleased with the volume of weekly work, believing the stack of worksheets and tests reflected solid learning.

Mr. Thompson needed to be in control, and he celebrated compliant students. He didn't value creativity, out-of-the-box thinking, problem-solving, or student talk. So why did parents lobby for their children to be in his class? Most likely, Mr. Thompson represented the kind of teaching many of them had experienced.

KEEPING INSTRUCTIONAL PRACTICES SIMPLY BECAUSE THEY WORKED FOR PARENTS AND TEACHERS ISN'T GOOD ENOUGH FOR TODAY'S STUDENTS.

DISCARD WHAT'S NOT WORKING

Students deserve better. Keeping instructional practices simply because they worked for parents and teachers isn't good enough for today's students. School leaders must expect better if they are to prepare students to be problem solvers, collaborators, and communicators. Mr. Thompson's story highlights some practices that definitely need to be reexamined and reimagined.

Extra credit. Although it's nice for students to bring tissues, pencils, and paper to class, a problem arises when the box of tissues changes a B on a math test to an A. The extra credit and adjusted grade don't reflect accurately what the student has learned and mastered. This type of extra credit needs to be eliminated. How do educators make this change to a familiar practice that many parents value?

Starting with a school's staff is important. We encourage staff to read and discuss articles to see extra credit in a new light. When teachers agree to change this practice, they can explain the school's position on this topic during parents' nights or back-to-school meetings. Schools also can explain to parents, through a podcast posted to the school's website, why extra credit to influence a grade doesn't offer an accurate picture of students' learning and progress. In situations where teachers don't agree to change the extra credit practice, administrators need to consider two avenues: Instead of choosing a top-down decision, they can encourage teachers to continue to read about and discuss the issue during the year. If most teachers agree to change by the end of the year, then it's possible to reach out to parents at the beginning of the following year. Administrators also can explain to staff that students are welcome to bring boxes of tissues and other items but doing so will no longer impact their grades.

Compliance. Although this may be an extreme example, we perceive Mr. Thompson's use of punishments and grades to enforce his goals to be similar to the message of Oliver Twist: children need to be submissive, follow rules, and comply with adults' demands. Compliance, however, does not support creativity, collaboration, communication, critical thinking, problem-solving, and making responsible choices—the skills students need to practice to be prepared for their future.

Engagement and motivation. In a compliant classroom such as Mr. Thompson's, children have limited opportunities to be engaged and motivated. Compliance puts the teacher at the center and in charge. This approach is not effective. Children come from diverse backgrounds, with diverse experiences, and with diverse levels of reading and writing expertise. A one-size-fits-all curriculum can't meet their needs. Students become engaged and motivated when they have choices, and when teachers offer learning experiences relevant to students' lives, experiences, and world.

Sorting and selecting students. A multiage classroom shouldn't be defined by a row of bookcases separating grade levels. If you take the same philosophical belief and apply it to heterogeneous classes, you can readily see that sorting and seating children by ability and test scores is unproductive. Some work, such as guided reading, is done with homogeneous groups, but other learning involves integrating students to tap into the dreams, stories, and prior knowledge each child brings to learning and problem-solving. Whether separated by age or by grade level, students benefit at times from collaborating and learning from each other. Relegating students to one group with little hope of change is not a best practice and hinders their motivation to improve. Flexible groups offer students multiple opportunities to move forward by learning with different peers.

MAKE LEARNING RELEVANT

Some of the work students complete in teacher-centered classes is inauthentic; it's not what adults do in the real world. These practices need to go because they make learning passive, and students need to be actively involved in everything they do at school. I (Evan) remember being bored in sixth-grade English because the teacher took half a year to read Tolkien's *The Hobbit* out loud. Every class ended with fifteen minutes of our copying notes explaining the symbolism, relationships among characters, and why Bilbo Baggins was heroic. As a result, my friends and I did not listen, and we learned very little about the art and skill of reading because the teacher did all the work. We just had to copy down what the teacher wanted us to know. Instead, students should be doing the work and actively participating during class time. The following practices need to change and become authentic to prepare students for college, career, and life.

Copying notes and worksheets. Instead of asking students to simply copy your notes, make note-taking authentic by modeling how to take notes. Don't assume that students know how to do this. Instead, invite students to talk first, and then write in their notebooks their responses to reading, watching a video, solving a math problem, or setting up and monitoring a science experiment. Students use their own words to capture and revise their thinking, and these words offer deep insights into what they do and don't understand. In addition, you can mine students' notebooks to inform mini-lessons on writing conventions or content for the whole class, small groups, or individual students.

Book reports. As an adult, have you ever written a report about a book you've read? The book report, a school-made genre, is often a long and boring retelling of an entire text. I (Laura) had students do oral book reports during my first year of teaching. It was painful to watch a student stand in front of the class and drone on and on about the book's plot. No thinking. No opinions. No connections. Moreover, these book reports bored the listening students.

Be authentic and develop a book review model appropriate for the age you teach. With colleagues, study book reviews found in newspapers and professional journals such as *The Horn Book* and *School Library Journal* or use a search engine to find samples of student book reviews. The purpose of book reviews is to evaluate and sell a beloved book to other readers—not to retell the story. Book reviews open with a brief summary, followed by the writer's opinion and reasons others should or shouldn't read the book. Students also can review books in podcasts, vlogs, and book trailers. Ask students to post these or written reviews on class and school websites for others to enjoy. This makes them real, purposeful, and powerful.

Round robin reading. Inviting students to take turns reading one to two paragraphs is not teaching for understanding and connecting information to other texts and current events. Many teachers claim they use this practice to ensure that students are reading. Unfortunately, there are pitfalls to this rationale. Reading aloud embarrasses students who struggle with the text, diminishing self-confidence and self-efficacy. Additionally, reading aloud does not improve students' ability to infer, analyze, connect, and respond emotionally. In fact, for students beyond the third grade, reading aloud actually slows them down, and they don't develop the silent reading expertise to cope with the reading demands of middle and high school. If accountability is a goal, first offer students materials they can read and learn from. Then engage them in paired and small group discussions, writing about reading and viewing topic-related videos. Confer with students and watch them to determine their progress and areas where they need additional support or reteaching.

Tests as the only assessments. We recognize that test-taking skills are relevant to life. Adults take tests for college admission, to obtain certification as a teacher, lawyer, doctor, or accountant, and to qualify for some jobs. However, we also believe students need more than test-taking skills and summative assessments to be successful. We encourage teachers and administrators to use formative assessments in addition to written tests. For example, students can prepare and present speeches, give book talks, perform impromptu plays, compose essays and stories, create and conduct surveys, design a website, hold interviews, and write news articles relating to topics they study.

REARRANGE FURNITURE TO REFLECT LEARNING EXPERIENCES

Authenticity in learning also extends to how teachers organize and arrange furniture in their classrooms. Flexible seating has become a consideration in many classrooms, and arrangement of furniture should reflect the kind of learning students are experiencing. When class seating arrangements are flexible and respond to the kinds of learning students do, the teacher and students can negotiate arrangements reflecting the diversity of their work. When we step into classes using flexible seating, we often see:

- A group working with the teacher at a table, and pairs of students on a rug sharing writing and discussing a book
- Some students working alone reading a self-selected book or using an app on a tablet
- A small group using technology for their project
- Two students writing on the "Wondering Wall" either questions about unclear information or words and topics they want to learn more about

In these classes, one-size-fits-all seating arrangements don't work because they aren't tuned in to how students learn or the diversity of learning.

Two questions have become our beacon for deciding whether seating arrangements and learning are authentic:

- Is the seating in concert with the instruction?
- Has the seating changed but the instruction remained the same?

Make student learning meaningful and relevant to their lives. Put students at the center of learning so they can build their own bank of stories and experiences and have the self-confidence to dream!

REFLECT! **DISCUSS WITH COLLEAGUES!** **REVISIT!**

- Reflect on some practices you would like to change and consider how you can work with colleagues to support these changes.
- Why does student-centered learning better prepare students for their future?

—— **Share your thoughts and ideas! #teammakers** ——

CHAPTER 5
COLLABORATING TO MAKE CHANGES

One of our favorite pastimes is dreaming about what schools will look like when they truly prepare students for their future. In fact, we spend a lot of time bouncing ideas off each other to develop our vision for more effective schools. Part of our vision is a greater amount of collaboration among educators and helping them feel empowered to discuss and eventually initiate much needed changes.

This is exemplified in the work Evan and his librarian, Mrs. Deem, did to transform the Johnson Williams Middle School library and the role of the librarian over the past few years. We believe their changes provide a model for how schools can collaborate and prepare students for their future. First, it's crucial to understand that change did not occur quickly; it took two years for the library to evolve. In fact, the goal is for it to evolve continually to meet the changing needs of teachers and students.

CREATE A PARTNERSHIP

Before the makeover, the library was fairly traditional, with a few spaces for students to read and an area for book displays. When Mrs. Deem and I (Evan) first met about this project, we agreed to create a list of what the space needed to become current as well as innovative into the future. Mrs. Deem shared ideas she had researched on the internet: makerspaces, a green screen for making videos, areas for silent reading, spaces ideal for students to collaborate on projects and discuss books, and a larger professional library for teachers. During our second meeting, we estimated the cost for the transition and prioritized our list of potential changes:

- Purchase recently published and relevant books
- Study technology needs
- Add makerspace materials
- Increase access to ebooks
- Order furniture more conducive to collaboration

Mrs. Deem, armed with myriad ideas from research, presented her dream library to our faculty and invited teachers to provide feedback and explore additional possibilities. The library makeover became a partnership between Mrs. Deem and the teachers with the common goal to transform the library into a hub of learning for staff and students. Over two school years, I budgeted funds so the librarian, with the teachers' enthusiastic support, could add several "diner" booths where students could discuss books and projects, and three exercise–reading bikes popular among students and staff. With Mrs. Deem's support, students and teachers made videos about the library's new spaces to post on our school website to raise enthusiasm among parents.

Mrs. Deem continually updated displays of new additions to the library and favorite genres and authors. She supported learning by helping teachers find books and materials for their subjects and projects. Communication and collaboration between Mrs. Deem and staff created a partnership, nudging teachers to explore using flexible seating and learning in their own classrooms. By visiting other classes already using flexible seating and reading about it on the internet, teachers realized that giving students choice and a voice in seating arrangements built trust between them and the teachers.

As we noted above, the process of transforming the Johnson Williams library into a media center exemplifies how school personnel can collaborate to bring about needed change. To facilitate productive and innovative change, keeping students' needs at the center, we recommend:

- Identifying a challenge
- Researching ideas and solutions
- Predicting costs
- Collaborating with staff to understand and revise

ANYONE CAN INITIATE CHANGE

Change can be initiated in a variety of ways by a variety of people, but it needs to be inclusive. Change doesn't have to start with the central office or school administrators. It can be a grassroots effort, initiated by staff or students. In Evan's school, the librarian initiated change in her space. Her research, communication, and collaboration with staff led to several teachers starting their own movement to explore flexible class arrangements and how they could create engaging learning environments for students. We encourage staff and students to initiate change in schools.

My (Laura) eighth-grade students started their own movement to initiate a change in their grade level. They complained about younger students having a mid-morning break and snack while they didn't. They told me, "We need a snack because we miss breakfast to sleep longer. When we're hungry, we think about eating and not learning."

I believe part of preparing students for their future is to honor reasonable requests and show them ways to bring about change, so I asked them, "What can you do to have a snack break put into your schedule?" This launched a movement among my students; groups collaborated to explore ways to reach their goal. During class they made and documented phone calls to local pediatricians, parents, and nutrition experts at our local hospital. They surveyed sixth- and seventh-grade students and those in another eighth-grade section. The students surveyed were unanimously in favor of a five- to ten-minute healthy snack break to include fruit, cheese and crackers, or protein bars. Students requested time to present their findings at a faculty meeting and elected two eighth-grade students to make their case. The students impressed the faculty with their research, their design, administration, and interpretation of the surveys, and their promise to eat healthy snacks.

The following week, the faculty notified students that there wasn't enough time in the current year's schedule to budget in a formal break; however, they could eat a snack during their second- or third-period classes while they completed tasks and at a time designated by their teachers. If the practice worked well, the faculty agreed to continue it the following year.

Student advocacy or leadership not only encourages students to raise their voices when they perceive a need for change, but it offers them opportunities to experience leadership. Ninth grader Leila Mohajer explains how student advocacy can create change:

SPEAK STUDENTS!
An Interlude by Leila Mohajer

All students should become familiar with student advocacy. Without it, teachers can't understand what their students are thinking or what they want. Students need to make their voices heard, and doing so is entirely in their hands. I'm sharing a real-life example to show the importance of student advocacy. My hope is teachers will use this to encourage student advocacy, and it will inspire students to advocate for themselves and others.

During an eighth-grade civics class, we had a whole unit covering student advocacy. Our teacher told us to choose from a list of current conflicts in our school, come up with a solution for the conflict, and present it to the class. Because of this experience, I was able to fully appreciate the way my cousin, Victoria Sander, advocated for herself when she faced a conflict at school.

Victoria, a sixth grader from North Carolina, had a major conflict with an English assignment, and the amount of time she was given to complete it. She was given three writing assignments but only one week to complete them. She told me, "I didn't know what to do. I had no time to do all three because of dance and my homework from other classes." She decided to take matters into her own hands and contacted her teacher.

Victoria respectfully explained to her teacher that she and her classmates felt they didn't have enough time to complete these assignments. On behalf of the whole class, she asked whether the deadline for the longer assignment could be pushed forward. Her teacher was very interested in this request and made a bargain with Victoria. If all the students received a passing grade on the first two assignments, the third assignment's deadline would be changed. However, if any of the students received a non-passing grade, the third assignment (which the students believed would take about three days to complete) would be due the following day. The students thought this was fair and after a class vote, they agreed to the incentive.

During the next class, the teacher announced that all the students had received a passing grade, so the longer assignment was not due until the end of the next week. Victoria mentioned that all her friends were thankful for her actions and appreciated her desire to speak up politely and help. Victoria used her voice to advocate not only for herself but for her entire class. The results were a great success for everyone.

STUDENT ADVOCACY OR LEADERSHIP NOT ONLY ENCOURAGES STUDENTS TO RAISE THEIR VOICES WHEN THEY PERCEIVE A NEED FOR CHANGE, BUT IT OFFERS THEM OPPORTUNITIES TO EXPERIENCE LEADERSHIP.

Students should never be afraid to advocate for themselves or speak up if they feel something can be improved. Advocacy is a very important skill to have, and it will enable students to advocate for causes throughout their lives.

ENCOURAGE ADVOCACY AND AGENCY

To rally staff around changes in instruction or flexible seating arrangements, and to improve communication among staff, students, and parents, we believe everyone—administrators, teachers, and students—should have an active role and voice in suggesting, exploring, and ultimately developing changes supporting students' learning. The school community is like the classroom: principals can develop an environment to encourage and respect suggestions for change just as teachers encourage students to negotiate seating, types of projects, and the amount of independent reading. Staff and students can shape a school's culture if administrators listen and take a collaborative leadership role in their school community. John Dewey said, "If we teach today's students as we taught yesterday, we rob them of tomorrow." Continually raising questions is an excellent way to identify areas your school should explore. Responding to questions should be school specific, because it ensures that changes enhance your school's culture and bring clarity to its vision.

QUESTIONS TO GENERATE INITIATIVES

Instead of offering definitive ideas for change or a one-size-fits-all solution, we invite staff and administrators to reflect on the following questions to develop school-wide initiatives to fit their school's culture and students. We encourage you to embrace differences among schools within the same district. Differences reflect community expectations, culture, climate, demographics, and students' needs. These questions can stir dreaming, spark research on possibilities, and prompt sharing stories and information. Use them as a springboard to spark meaningful changes in your school.

- What does a walk-through in your building reveal about the learning and teaching going on in classes?
- What kinds of professional learning are in place? How can you improve these?
- Does your school media center have a section for teachers that is stocked with professional books and journals?
- How does your school library illustrate that it is more than simply a place to check out and return books?
- How does your principal support professional learning?
- Do teachers have common beliefs about children and learning?
- Do teachers collaborate and communicate to ensure they are working on and meeting common goals for students?
- How does technology enhance students' learning?
- How do teachers, administrators, and students use technology to communicate with each other, parents, and the community?
- Are all students reading books and materials they understand? Can they understand and learn from all books used for all subjects?
- How do faculty, team, and department meetings advance your school's vision?

We hope these questions generate additional questions, so schools continually look at teaching practices, students' learning, intervention, relationships, flexible grouping and seating, professional learning, and ways to communicate with all stakeholders. When schools squarely place students at the center, they can better prepare them for their future, because instead of covering curriculum, teachers work diligently to meet each student's needs. Administrators, teachers, and students will continue to foster change as they collaborate and communicate and reimagine learning. They should not leave their creative thinking, dreams, and stories at the school's entrance. We challenge you to become TeamMakers and invite all members of your school community to bring these tools to school to encourage innovative changes in every learning space, engage in collaborative conversations, and break free of what holds you back.

REFLECT! DISCUSS WITH COLLEAGUES! REVISIT!

- How can collaboration create meaningful changes?
- How is your leadership encouraging or discouraging teacher and student advocacy?

—— **Share your thoughts and ideas! #teammakers** ——

CHAPTER 6
REDEFINING CENTRAL OFFICE ROLES

For schools to become learning centers that can effectively prepare students for the future, traditional leadership roles should be redefined by risk-taking and creative thinking. We believe these traits are necessary for school leaders to successfully navigate the known problems schools face today and the unknown issues they will face in the future. Administrators, teachers, and parents need to become daring yet intentional risk-takers and then offer children opportunities to take their own risks to cope with their unknowns.

"I'M GONNA JUMP!"

Evan and I love the "Girls' First Ski Jump" video on YouTube. It is a great reminder of how risk-taking can initially raise fear and uncertainty but ultimately produce enthusiasm and courage. Standing at the top of the jump, the girl gives herself a pep talk, saying, "It's no big deal. I can do it! I'm gonna jump." But then she asks questions to delay the moment of commitment. Her fear is palpable. However, when she successfully navigates the jump, she shouts, "It's so fun! It seems like nothing now!" and gives herself a triumphant cheer! It was tough for this girl to imagine she could survive the jump—much less love it! But she learned this truth: Fear and courage often walk hand in hand. Once she took the plunge and experienced success and sheer joy, her courage and pleasure grew while her fear faded!

FEAR AND COURAGE OFTEN WALK HAND IN HAND.

We believe educators would benefit from a similar experience. Because fear of change is linked to fear of the unknown, perhaps change comes slowly in education when leaders are reluctant to step into unfamiliar territory. But if they adopt a willingness to take risks, like Columbus and Magellan or John Glenn and Mae Jemison, the first African American woman in space, who braved the unknown and changed the world, school leaders will infuse their districts with an exploring mindset and change the education world.

A thought leader on Digital Leadership with the International Center for Leadership in Education, Eric Sheninger's words resonate with a key mission of TeamMakers: "It's not our future we are preparing students for, but theirs. We can ill afford to prepare them for a world that won't exist." As we mentioned earlier, many ideas educators valued and implemented in the past don't work today and won't work in the future. Technology alone can't create the needed changes. How educators conceive of learning, use technology, and shift their own thinking through risk-taking is what will change children's lives! We encourage you to harness your courage and leap into the unknown to rethink leadership and learning and discover better ways to create deeply connected school districts.

THE CENTRAL OFFICE

Central office personnel need to become more connected with all members of a school district, and this can happen when they are more visible, are building relationships, and are taking advantage of collaborative opportunities with staff and families. We recognize that some elements of central office administrators' roles require them to be in their offices, but their roles also necessitate that they be connected to their district's schools. We believe these connections best occur within the schools.

I (Evan) have taught in school districts where the superintendent was virtually invisible. Principals and staff heard the superintendent share a vision at the convocation opening the school year, but, unfortunately, the visibility often ended there. I have also worked in school districts where the superintendents and their assistants made it a priority to visit classrooms to build relationships with teachers and students. At the start of the school year, they added time to their schedules to visit schools a few times a week and observe teaching in action during sports, choir, band, and content subjects. They did more than a walkthrough; they spent the time needed to understand the learning and offered positive feedback, personally or through a follow-up email the same day they visited.

THE SUPERINTENDENT

I (Laura) have consulted in schools with "invisible" superintendents like Evan describes. But I have also worked with Dr. Jason Van Heukelum, Superintendent of Winchester Public Schools, who mirrors the changes and risk-taking leadership Evan and I want to see. Dr. Van Heukelum continued to teach math when he ran a kindergarten through twelfth grade American school in Bolivia. In fact, he continues to teach math currently as the superintendent of the Winchester Schools. Starting in January 2018, Dr. Van Heukelum taught small groups of seventh graders every Thursday. He experienced firsthand the pressure of standardized tests and the resulting struggle teachers face regarding curriculum: do they engage students in authentic tasks or put more time into covering material needed for students to score higher on annual state tests?

Working in classes enables Dr. Van Heukelum to gauge the feelings of teachers and students. He plans his schedule and visits every school every week of the year. On one of those visits, he spent time in an intervention class called Pathways that I was teaching with two English language arts (ELA) teachers—a class of twenty-four students reading three to five years below fifth-grade level. While Dr. Van Heukelum's financial support of the division's reading initiative has provided class libraries and choice genre units of study, he also personally impacts teachers and students, as I observed on this occasion.

When he entered the class, the teachers and I were leading guided reading groups. Students not in a group were reading self-selected books, looking for an independent reading book, or having a quiet conversation about a book with a peer partner. While observing the guided reading groups, Dr. Van Heukelum asked teachers and students questions and shared positive observations. He talked to students about their independent reading, and they eagerly shared thoughts and feelings.

After he left, an upbeat buzz whisked through the class like a mini windstorm: the superintendent cared about their reading! Teachers felt valued, and his visit inspired them to work harder to improve their students' reading. The positive relationship that started during this visit continued through follow-up interactions between the superintendent and these teachers and students.

Believing building relationships and getting into the teaching trenches support his efforts as superintendent, Dr. Van Heukelum also organized three student advisory groups: one at the intermediate school, one at the middle school, and one at the high school. Dr. Van Heukelum invited teachers to make recommendations for students to attend advisory meetings but instructed that the students needed to represent the school community's demographics and range of academic achievement. He told me that his goal was to meet with students twice per year and take the pulse of the districts' schools through candid conversations with them.

Dr. Van Heukelum also conceived the Innovation Center, a maverick initiative allowing high school students to learn academics through technical education. For example, students can earn a high school math credit in conjunction with welding or a chemistry credit while studying health science. This integrated learning consists of in-depth, multi-week projects requiring individual students to master content and collaborative applications. Students' experiences mirror the workplace as they manage projects, negotiate time needed for completion, and experience personal and collaborative learning. The goal of the Innovation Center is to "develop life-ready graduates who are highly skilled, self-directed, and community-minded." This out-of-the-box thinking that Dr. Van Heukelum demonstrated is a model of how a superintendent can build relationships among all stakeholders and collaborate with school leaders to develop initiatives to prepare students for their tomorrows. We hope every superintendent will follow his lead and be bold, be daring, and take risks.

DIRECTOR OF INSTRUCTION

Another central office role we dream of redefining is the director of instruction (or content area director), and we believe that "instruction" and risk-taking should define the position. While we were discussing this book with Shelley Burgess, she revealed that she had been a director of instruction for a school district. In this role, she was continually out of the office, observing classes in every school and discussing her observations with teachers. She explained that this was the only way she could understand what instruction looked like in different schools. Shelley's practice makes sense to us! In fact, it models our vision of educators taking risks and sharing stories, hopes, and dreams to lead to meaningful change.

Recently, I (Laura) was training middle school teachers in the Wantagh School District on Long Island to transform their ELA classes into reading–writing workshops. Dr. Marc Ferris, Assistant Superintendent of Instruction, fully participated with the teachers and, on the one occasion when he had to slip out to attend a meeting, the superintendent took his place. Central office administrators learning beside teachers, a first for most of the teachers—who valued and enjoyed the experience—quickly demonstrated how much the central office supported moving to a workshop model. Equally important, the experience helped Dr. Ferris understand the need to fund class libraries and books for units of study so students could self-select books for instructional and independent reading.

In many school districts, the directors of instruction spend far more days in meetings and completing forms for federal and state departments of education than they spend in classrooms. Fortunately, Dr. Ferris is one who redefines this role, working closely with principals, teachers, and students who have become TeamMakers.

WE ARE IN THIS TOGETHER
An Interlude by Marc Ferris, EdD

Since I became a central office administrator, my definition of this role continues to evolve. As a middle school principal, I was happy when central office types left me alone to work with my teachers and students. I thought I knew what my school needed, and my desire to learn more and improve the instructional practice within my team was unwavering. We did great instructional work and could see its immediate impact with our students. However, when I became an assistant superintendent for instruction, my focus changed dramatically. I immediately realized that, although a single building could do great work, a tremendous amount of the work is lost if the entire district isn't moving forward together, focusing on the same larger instructional goals for student learning.

As a new assistant superintendent, I was a fish out of water. No teachers or students were near my office, and every interaction with school building people was through email, a phone call, or a large cabinet meeting to cover a to-do list weighing us down. I found myself sneaking into the middle school to help students with their locker woes. Clearly, leaving my building had left me feeling a sense of loss. And although helping sixth graders with locker jams was momentarily satisfying, it was not my prime objective in my new central office role. I realized I could not make a difference in district-wide instructional practice simply through emails, formal administrative cabinet meetings, or fixing jammed lockers.

Instead, my superintendent and I formed a research team, inviting teachers, students, and administrators to participate and study our district with a critical lens. Eighteen teachers representing each of the five schools in the district, two AP capstone students, and eight administrators spent several hours per week designing the study.

I felt alive again! I was learning and collaborating with a group who shared a common goal! We designed research questions, online surveys, and focus groups for parents, teachers, students, and all district staff. Our mission was to uncover the district's values, strengths, weaknesses, and hopes for the future. Not only were we doing valuable work together, I was also building important relationships with a core group of teachers and administrators.

Through this team experience, we discovered that learning and working together as a team is important, and the process taught us that no one role is more valuable than another. We struggled and laughed together throughout our teamwork. Learning is both difficult *and* rewarding. Together we analyzed the data and presented two hundred pages of findings to the Board of Education, along with a five-year shared instructional plan for the entire district.

Fast forward to today. I still help middle school students with their lockers. I also walk kindergarten students to their classrooms on the first day of school, help with bus drills when needed, cover a class or two when subs aren't available, and guest teach for the AP capstone class at least once a year. These may not be my "official" duties, but this sends an important message to the school community that we are all in this together.

Another way I communicate this team attitude is by attending instructional trainings. I love to learn, and I want our teachers to see that learning is fun and joyful, and it helps us stay sane in the classroom. I always sit with the teachers rather than in the back corner watching over them like the "instructional police." I encourage other administrators to do the same; otherwise they're separating "admin" from "real folks," and this makes everyone nervous!

When the teachers are asked to turn and talk to each other, I do so with them. When teaching moves are practiced, I do them too. At first, the teachers are terrified, wondering, "Why is this guy sitting with me and talking to me? Is something wrong?" Fairly quickly, though, they see I genuinely love to learn and want to improve my own understanding of teaching methodology while supporting them in their learning. Participating also allows me to hear from the teacher's perspective any challenges when they are raised—perhaps they need more funds for books, or a roadblock removed. Better yet, I'm able to respond to assure teachers that their concerns have been heard. *I can do that! The principal and I are on it!* And when teachers start getting nervous about making changes because of state testing, I can reinforce with all my heart and soul from a central office position:

"Stop thinking about STATE TESTS! You have our permission and encouragement do whatever needed to help you be successful with your students. We are here for you!"

This type of response may seem risky to some, but to me, it's the essence of being human. As I finished my first year as an assistant superintendent for instruction, my biggest takeaway was related to this idea. When I act like a human being, demonstrate care and concern for others, show my love and passion for learning, and roll up my sleeves hoping to get to "the needs and challenges" with teachers and staff, everyone starts moving forward together. Educators working *together* is when the true magic happens.

REDEFINING COLLABORATION

Warren G. Bennis, who has authored several books on leadership, said, "Leadership is the capacity to translate vision into reality." Our vision is for central office administrators to be risk-takers and redefine their traditional roles. We believe this can be done only through greater collaboration among the superintendent, assistants, school principals, and other school leaders on district-wide initiatives affecting all schools. Although face-to-face meetings are preferable for building relationships, we recognize that the scope of these administrative jobs often limits the time people have. Fortunately, this creates another opportunity for risk-taking.

Technology can be used to forge relationships when time does not permit a personal visit. For example, it's possible to Skype from your office with a group collaborating on an initiative. Make a short "fireside chat" video to post on the district's website to explain a decision to teachers and parents or to generate enthusiasm for a district-wide initiative or to communicate appreciation and thanks to staff, students, and school administrators. This may be a new way for some to communicate, but technology holds the potential to help leaders better connect with members of their school communities. If you're a central office administrator, we encourage you to step out, take the risk, and try it!

Superintendents and directors of instruction must be open to change when needed. Their flexibility can lead them to reflect on opportunities for change and growth and embrace what is critical to

TECHNOLOGY CAN BE USED TO FORGE RELATIONSHIPS WHEN TIME DOES NOT PERMIT A PERSONAL VISIT.

the school district—even when it requires taking a risk. Followers often accept the status quo, but the leader continually asks why and quickly moves toward change. As a central office administrator, be the one who redefines your role, transforming challenges into positive opportunities to revise your district's narrative.

- How can redefining the roles of the superintendent and director of instruction positively impact teaching practices and students' learning?

- Reflect on your position and its connections to your school district, then ask how relationships can improve between central office staff and schools. Discuss observed strengths and areas needing improvement.

—— **Share your thoughts and ideas! #teammakers** ——

CHAPTER 7
REDEFINING SCHOOL
LEADERSHIP ROLES

For schools to become the learning centers needed to effectively prepare students for their future, not only do central office roles need to be redefined, but the roles of building-level leadership also have to be redefined. Although their specific responsibilities are different, risk-taking and creative thinking are equally important to the success of these leaders. In addition, relationship-building and fostering advocacy or leadership among teachers and students also play an important part in redefining the roles of school leaders. Fortunately, many building leaders are making positive changes.

The principal's role has changed dramatically since I (Evan) was in elementary and middle school. I attended an independent school, and I remember the headmaster speaking briefly at assemblies. Teachers also sent students to his office to be punished for misbehaving, breaking important rules, or consistently not turning in homework. This is the sum of my recollection of the school's leader during my first two years in middle school. I didn't know him personally or have a relationship with him. However, this changed when I was in the eighth grade because we met once a week in his office to discuss moral dilemmas. My classmates and I enjoyed the discussions—especially because there was no grade or homework! Because of this class, I also developed a relationship with the headmaster, and I still carry good memories of our group conversations.

Today, whether in public, independent, or charter schools, students and teachers often interact with the principal and assistant principal in the cafeteria, library, during classes, when students arrive at and depart from school, and at sports, theater, and music events. Relationships between the building leaders, school staff, and students are a foundation for a healthy school culture.

As a principal, I (Evan) am always looking for new ways to model and build relationships by connecting better with my staff and students. Recently, I gave my cell phone and walkie-talkie to my assistant principal and became an eighth-grade student for a day, attending

FIND WAYS TO BUILD RELATIONSHIPS WITH STUDENTS AND STAFF AND, ULTIMATELY, DEVELOP A POSITIVE SCHOOL COMMUNITY.

classes and eating lunch in the cafeteria with my "classmates." I quickly learned that switching gears and moving from subject to subject was extremely challenging, and I felt tired at the end of the day. But it was worth it! One student summed up the feelings of others when he said, "I really got to know you, Mr. Robb, and feel comfortable talking to you anytime now." Through our bond of common experiences and my willingness to listen to and respect their ideas during the school day, these eighth graders and I developed a trusting relationship.

As students, staff, and parents experience the care of their principals, relationships develop, ensuring a path of loyalty among the school community. During the school day, effective principals are out of their offices more than they are behind a closed door. They attend meetings, observe classes, conduct walk-throughs, stroll through the halls when students change classes, and visit with staff, students, and parents. To make herself more visible and accessible to students and teachers on hall duty, Holly Rushner, a principal of a middle school in Virginia, purchased a desk on wheels and, several days a week, spends two hours in different hallways interacting with students and teachers. Her computer sits on her mobile desk, and she can complete some work during lulls. Effective leaders, like Rushner, find ways to build relationships with students and staff and, ultimately, develop a positive school community.

COACHING PRINCIPALS

Because school leadership is important, we envision school districts coaching their principals to improve the teaching and learning in schools. Marta W. Aldrich discusses this at Chalkbeat.org (August 2018), and we agree this is a creative approach to meaningful change, one aligning with our vision of deeper collaboration and connections among leaders in school districts.

Traditionally, principals' professional learning consists of workshops and trainings on administrative and operational issues. Coaching has not been included. However, according to Aldrich's study, coaching is the way to improve schools and align their cultures with the district-wide vision and mission, whether the principal is a first-year leader or a seasoned veteran. In this study, central office supervisors who were previously principals embraced the role of coach, but we also believe that experienced principals should coach less-experienced principals in their district. Effective and intentional coaching not only helps the person being coached but also supports the coach as both participants reflect on and articulate what they learned and how it transfers into positive actions.

Coaching with an emphasis on reflection, communication, and relationship building puts fresh eyes on instruction and learning and has the potential to:
- Help principals set priorities and refocus their commitment on improving teaching and learning
- Build trusting relationships
- Develop curricula to prepare students and staff for their futures
- Support teacher advocacy as a form of leadership growing out of what teachers do every day

TEACHER ADVOCACY

When teachers collaborate to effect change, develop professional learning communities, and continually revisit core curricula to make sure the content responds to all students' needs, they embrace shared leadership roles. I (Laura) experienced the power of teacher advocacy the first year I worked as a consultant-teacher at Daniel Morgan Intermediate School, teaching fifth-grade students who were reading one-and-a-half to four or more years below grade level.

Three other teachers, part of the fifth-grade ELA team, and I wanted an extra class to support these striving readers. However, the principal was new and wasn't convinced that replacing one of the students' two electives with an additional reading class would work. Continual discussions and our dogged persistence resulted in an agreement to schedule an extra daily reading class. Administrators and teachers agreed to monitor progress carefully. If students didn't improve by the end of the year, they would look for other solutions.

To obtain buy-in and support, the teachers called parents and spoke with children, carefully explaining why they were losing an elective as well as the purpose of the extra reading instruction. In addition to their original sixty minutes of reading and language arts, these students would have an extra seventy-three minutes of reading instruction including a daily interactive and instructional "read aloud," an opportunity to build fluency by practicing reading and performing self-selected poems, and time for guided and independent reading. Students always self-selected books, with teachers repeatedly modeling how to choose a book.

The ELA and Pathways *curriculum* was successful because the school district provided funds for six hundred books in each fifth-grade classroom library. The school also purchased genre and theme-based books for reading units in ELA classes. However, the *students* were successful because of the teachers who used their leadership skills to advocate for the children's needs, enabling them to make one to two years' progress in reading instructional levels.

As a principal, I (Evan) believe in collaborative teacher leadership to support students' learning and teachers' professional growth. In fact, teacher advocacy needs to be one of the principal's core beliefs for schools to embrace the concept and make it a part of their mission. When the principal builds trusting relationships with teachers, encourages them to take risks, and respects their ideas and suggestions, the power of teacher advocacy becomes part of the school's environment. Additionally, it is critical for principals to foster reflection, use research-based best practices, and wisely offer specific praise in conversations, emails, and handwritten notes to affirm these good practices. To encourage growth, principals can address specific adjustments when staff needs to improve and support them to move forward.

Set aside time at teacher, team, and department meetings to discuss organic leadership opportunities, evolving from the daily work they do with students and colleagues. I invite teachers to take on a leadership role by using pineapple charts. Developed by Jennifer Gonzalez and Mark Barnes, a pineapple chart is a grid containing an empty square for each individual class period during the week. Charts are posted in a common area, such as next to teachers' mailboxes or in the faculty room. Teachers jot down an exciting lesson in the square corresponding to when they'll teach it, and interested colleagues can arrange to observe their lesson. In addition to the pineapple chart, consider these other suggestions for teacher advocacy:

- Create an advocacy group for professional learning, using social media, book studies, and sharing articles and student work.
- Organize grade-level groups to identify the most effective interventions for students.
- Be inclusive and invite colleagues to study scheduling issues and suggest changes to the principal. The more teachers and staff you include in an advocacy group, the greater the reach for your message and ideas. Moreover, as the reach increases, you empower more staff and the greater the diversity of feedback you receive on issues.
- Form a group to review curriculum and ensure that core content responds to students' needs. Learn more about differentiation.
- Organize a professional book study or a study of literature appropriate to a grade level.

Remember to extend invitations, rather than issue mandates. Invitations imply choice and can develop a team of teacher leaders who support school administrators and become catalysts for positive change in your school and district. As teacher advocates strengthen their own growth mindset and collective efficacy, they also model leadership skills for their students.

STUDENTS AS LEADERS

I (Evan) remember first learning about leadership in the third grade when I collaborated with classmates to run a business called The Virginia Company. Our class prepared and sold lemonade every day to all kindergarten through fifth-grade students. We worked on teams, but the teams changed throughout the year so everyone experienced each aspect of the business: counting orders, preparing and delivering cups of lemonade, ordering lemonade mix and cups based on demand, and helping our teacher keep clear records. Mrs. Morgoglione, our teacher, trusted us and encouraged us to work in teams. She gave us the opportunity to experience leadership, listen to different ideas and opinions, and experience the delight of seeing a profit from our small business. When administrators support student leadership and give students a meaningful voice at school, they cultivate the skills needed for successful leadership. We believe students of all ages can benefit from opportunities to experience and acquire leadership. You may want to consider some of the suggestions below.

PRIMARY AND ELEMENTARY GRADES

- **Fundraising.** Young children raise money by making and selling cards for Valentine's Day, Christmas, and Easter. The money is used to support a charity, to purchase books for their class, or to help families in their community.
- **Class librarians.** Place young students in charge of making sure library books are signed out properly and put back when returned.
- **Materials persons**. Have students hand out paper, pencils, crayons, scissors, and tape.
- **Recess leaders.** Students are in charge of bringing sports and play equipment to recess and returning it to its proper place afterward.
- **Class communicators.** Students write thank you notes and birthday greetings to classmates.
- **Morning announcement teams.** Students can recommend a favorite book, make announcements of upcoming events, and welcome guests.

MIDDLE AND HIGH SCHOOL GRADES

- **Student government.** Students participate in school government groups throughout the year. Not only is it important for student government representatives to meet regularly, but they should also debrief each semester to reflect on accomplishments as well as future projects and issues to tackle.
- **Advisory councils.** Staff select students to meet monthly or bimonthly with school administrators to enable the administrators to understand students' feelings about classes and school life. The students serving on this council can change each quarter or twice a year and should represent the demographics and academic ranges of the school.
- **Ambassadors.** Faculty choose students to guide parents through the school on conference days and help new students during their orientation period. At my (Evan) school, ambassadors also put positive notes on students' lockers to celebrate a peer's work and accomplishments.
- **Community-minded clubs.** Students raise money to give to community causes or needs such as eyeglasses for students, supplies for the local animal shelter, and food for the homeless.
- **Student news team.** Students work with the principal to present a special newscast on video to be posted to the school's website. At my (Evan) school, we continue to refine and adjust the roles of this team, who prepare newscasts with my support. One student interviews teachers; one reports sports news; another discusses upcoming events; and one highlights happenings in different areas of the school, such as the library, cafeteria, band and art rooms, or gym.

By nurturing students' leadership skills, principals invite them to focus on issues and needs to make a difference in their school and surrounding community. Students have opportunities to develop independence, agency, and responsibility, as well as to make choices and decisions while collaborating and communicating with staff and peers. Principals who value leadership and creative thinking in staff and students open the door for these groups to become an important part of leadership initiatives. Through one-on-one interactions and by collaborating with others, principals model positive leadership and encourage teacher and student leadership opportunities.

- Why is it important for principals to encourage teacher advocacy?
- How do leadership opportunities support students' development of leadership skills?

—— **Share your thoughts and ideas! #teammakers** ——

PART III
Becoming a Community of Problem Solvers

To become a district-wide community of problem solvers who band together and rally around initiatives benefiting all schools, we suggest instructional and learning practices school districts need to discuss. Evan and I view these practices as the pillars of support and networking in schools ready to position themselves as TeamMakers who continually assess and refine their school's culture. To accomplish this, we recommend developing a depth of communication within and between schools and between the central office and schools.

Evan and I address how mentors acculturate new teachers into a school, providing the support and guidance necessary to reduce stress and make their first year a resounding success. We also discuss the need for coaches who partner with teachers to improve instruction and provide the emotional support necessary to implement instructional changes.

Coaches can help build schools filled with skilled and exemplary teachers who use a student-centered approach in their classes. Students who learn in such classes have daily opportunities to practice the skills needed to become future problem solvers: collaboration, communication through talk and writing, as well as creative and critical thinking. Learning for students is active, as they use inquiry to drive their reading, reflection, and understanding. In addition, relationships become important in student-centered classes. Positive and trusting relationships among and between administrators, teachers, and students set the emotional stage for taking risks that can lead to innovation. The problem solvers Evan and I hope schools can develop take risks, think out of the box, and use analytical thinking to develop unique solutions.

We've broadened the idea of problem solvers to include students, teachers, staff, and all administrators. Now there's an extended group who collaborate, cultivate, and value positive relationships, communicate, and analyze issues. As a result, these TeamMakers have better positioned and equipped themselves to meet future challenges.

CHAPTER 8
MENTORS AND COACHES

As Evan and I continue to build the picture of schools becoming learning centers that prepare students for the future, skilled teachers will be a key part of this goal. One way to ensure that schools continually work to develop effective and knowledgeable teachers is through mentoring and coaching.

Before beginning consulting and training third- through eighth-grade teachers, I (Laura) had breakfast with their superintendent and director of instruction, who raised a challenge they faced. Annually, a few new hires left after their first or second year, and for the past two years, the number of departing new teachers had increased. Both administrators feared this would become a pattern unless they intervened. The administrators described their "new teacher program" as three days packed with reviewing the faculty handbook and lists for lunch, recess, and hall duties. In addition, new teachers learned procedures for taking attendance and completing report cards and forms for repeated student absences and tardiness. Not surprising to me, exit interviews with departing teachers revealed, along with the challenges of managing their classes, that they felt overwhelmed with procedures.

"Do you have a mentoring program?" I asked. When they both replied "no" and wanted to learn more about mentoring, I offered to set aside time at the end of each day of workshops to discuss the benefits of mentoring with them and their teachers. As we met over the next few days, the group agreed that they would benefit from a school mentoring program and that teachers should be involved in developing it.

Over time, principals met with teacher volunteers to develop a mentoring program fitting their school's needs. Administrators soon recognized that the tradition of dumping lots of information onto new teachers only added to their confusion and frustration. Mentoring would slow down the learning process, enabling new teachers to absorb and apply information as needs arose.

It's fine for school districts to reserve time before the start of the school year to provide new teachers with information needed to successfully navigate their first two weeks in the classroom. In addition, when meetings combine relationship building and information, they can spark support among new teachers and between teachers and administrators. They also tell teachers that administrators care about them and are happy to have them on board.

SUPPORT FROM MENTORS CAN REDUCE ANXIETY AND GROW TRUSTING RELATIONSHIPS FOR FIRST-YEAR TEACHERS AND EVEN MORE EXPERIENCED TEACHERS WHO ARE NEW TO A SCHOOL.

MENTORING FOR SUCCESS

Mentoring is an effective way to acclimate teachers to a new school's procedures, values, and beliefs. A mentor is a formal partner for a new teacher who supports that teacher throughout the school year. Mentorship varies, and, like many coaching models, each school's program adjusts to the needs of its staff. The primary goal of mentors is to help new teachers adjust to how their school works. Effective mentors are proactive, supporting teachers in their moment of need before they reach the point of frustration. Other responsibilities might include helping teachers navigate school practices and procedures, offering reminders for recess, lunch, or bus duties, assisting with the setup of a grade book, pointing out important school dates, or identifying the formative assessments to compile for IEP (individualized education plan) meetings. They can offer suggestions for coping with student behavior problems affecting learning. Although communication between mentors and new teachers can be done through email or texts, at team and department meetings, and during common planning times, we believe face-to-face conversations promote deeper understanding of procedures and develop better relationships. Support from mentors can reduce anxiety and grow trusting relationships for first-year teachers and even more experienced teachers who are new to a school.

Mentorship is important, and I (Evan) encourage teachers to volunteer to be mentors even though it might occasionally require carving out extra time before or after school to meet with mentees. The first few years of teaching can be hard, and mentorship makes a difference in the success curve of new teachers. When principals reach out for mentors, I suggest that they consider offering a list of mentoring responsibilities, perhaps including some of those listed below. However, it's also important for them list the qualities of a good mentor. Mentors should be:

- **Effective.** They should understand the mission and vision of the school.
- **Organized.** They must be able to scaffold important school procedures.
- **Empathetic and compassionate**. Mentors need to be able to step into the shoes of anxious or confused new teachers and smooth their worries through explanations and timely reminders of due dates.
- **Upbeat and positive.** When communicating needs and affirming the progress observed in teachers via personal conversation, email, or text, mentors should always use constructive words.
- **Approachable.** Mentors are available when a teacher experiences challenges, confusion, or doesn't know how to support a student or tackle an instructional challenge.
- **Active listeners.** Mentors should respond to what a teacher says in an honest and caring manner.

When I meet with teachers who have volunteered to become mentors, I explain that they can impact new teachers' success by helping them have a positive transition to our school's culture, practices, traditions, and procedures. Mentoring new teachers not only supports those teachers but also increases the likelihood of their students having a successful year!

COACHING

After their first year or two in a new school, some teachers might need instructional support that is beyond what volunteer mentors have time to do. These teachers require guidance from instructional coaches, who can provide deeper and broader support to colleagues who face ongoing challenges or need to make improvements in a specific area. Because of this, to be an effective instructional coach requires experience, expertise in a specific area such as literacy, and a greater time commitment.

Several years ago, I (Laura) worked as a coach in a middle school, and I suggested to the principal that I invite teachers to work with me. The teachers and I would discuss desired outcomes and plan our coaching agenda. The principal agreed—and in fact, he had one teacher in mind for special coaching. He wanted to "save" Mr. Sadler, a veteran teacher who had recently submitted a letter of resignation after investing twenty-five years teaching at this middle school. Mr. Sadler didn't want to change from using a basal reading program and worksheets to using the finest books in a reading workshop. I expressed to the principal my reluctance to work with Mr. Sadler, pointing out that effective coaching required a dual commitment. However, the principal's insistence finally wore me down, and I agreed to try.

I knew developing a relationship with Mr. Sadler was critical. He turned out to have a great sense of humor and shared memorable stories about his second life as a singer in a small band. However, despite a few enjoyable conversations over a cup of coffee, I could not convince Mr. Sadler to invest in organizing a reading–writing workshop. We both enjoyed chatting. However, he honestly didn't want to change. "Too much work at my stage of teaching," he explained. "Time to move on to something else."

I felt sad about Mr. Sadler's decision and believed I had failed him and the principal. But reflection and conversations with Evan reminded me that coaching can't be forced on a teacher. Because the goal of coaching is to improve instruction, the coach and the teacher must commit to a lengthy process for positive changes in teaching and learning practices to occur.

Teachers need the coach's support to change and adjust their instructional practices and to cultivate the habit of reading professional materials to enlarge their knowledge of how children learn. In my (Evan) school, a coach or coaching team may focus on some teachers with school initiatives for the year, such as differentiation, reading-writing workshops, or developing a student-centered approach. Some districts have enough money to hire one to three full-time instructional coaches for each school, though tight budgets have caused many school districts to reduce their number or eliminate coaching positions altogether. Because budgets are almost always tight—and coaching is so important—explore the possibility of creating a half-time teacher and half-time coach position to ensure that coaching is available to teachers.

Another important role of coaches is to help promote buy-in among teachers who need to change instructional practices. Although the principal has the authority to mandate change, this rarely inspires people or instills feelings of caring and commitment. When teachers lack the background knowledge for changes and don't have a mental model of what the changes will look like in their classrooms, top-down mandates won't work. Moreover, top-down decisions don't build the collective buy-in needed for changes to be effective. Coaches are a valuable resource in this buy-in process. They can help communicate and promote the changes necessary for educators to learn, problem solve, and positively impact students for the future. We discourage mandates and positional authority as a strategy for substantive change and, instead, encourage schools to build a collective understanding and appreciation of the value of coaching.

Requests for coaching can come from a teacher personally asking for help, an administrator suggesting change, or parents communicating that a teacher needs support. I (Laura) recall a first-year teacher who struggled teaching fifth-grade science. Her class consisted of students completing worksheet packets and memorizing new vocabulary for weekly unit tests aligned with the state's content requirements. By December the principal's concerns, combined with those of knowledgeable parents, nudged the principal to assign a coach to the teacher for one semester.

The coach, Ms. Bates, started a conversation with the teacher by asking two questions about science: *What do scientists do?* and *How do they think about information and topics?* Ms. Bates followed up with a third question: *How can you help your students think and learn like scientists and make their experiences relevant to their lives?* Over nine weeks, with the daily support of her coach, the teacher abandoned boring worksheets and began integrating technology and opportunities for students to reflect on their learning. Students set up experiments to test hypotheses and collaborated to discuss observations and share conclusions and reflections.

Nine weeks, however, usually isn't enough time to create in-depth changes to instructional practices. Progress through coaching takes time, because the process of change is not linear but recursive, moving backward, surging ahead, or staying in a holding pattern. Although pleased with the teacher's progress, Ms. Bates reduced her time in the teacher's classes to three times per week over the next nine weeks, and then to twice per week afterward. This gradual release of responsibility enabled her to monitor how the teacher fared on her own and determine whether she had absorbed the changes in practice to the extent she could implement them herself.

A trusting relationship developed between the science teacher and Ms. Bates, in part because the principal made it clear their relationship was confidential. The principal didn't require the coach to report her observations because he trusted her and encouraged the professional coaching relationship. When the principal trusts his or her coaches, constant updates aren't needed. A sensitive and knowledgeable coach knows when a teacher has enough confidence to invite administrators into the classroom and can encourage the teacher to extend the invitation to an administrator to observe lessons.

TEACHERS WHO COACH

Coaches need to have enough teaching experience as well as the skills required to collaborate, create, think critically, and use a student-centered approach within a workshop environment. Although we have observed school districts inviting teachers to coach after two to three years in the classroom, we believe teachers need more time teaching and learning from their students to become effective coaches, confident enough to support other teachers. We also believe it's important for coaches to continue teaching one class throughout the year. I (Laura) did this when I was an instructional coach. In fact, I continue to teach today to learn from my students, but also to experience and be empathetic to the challenges teachers face with planning, differentiating instruction, finding resources and materials, reaching students with a wide range of reading levels, integrating technology to enhance learning, and communicating with parents.

Effective coaches are curious and ask questions—of themselves and the teachers they coach—leading to reflection and possibly sparking the need to learn more about a teaching practice or content subject. Questions lead to negotiating priorities and identifying what the coaches and teachers will collaborate on. They also can reduce the coaches' urge to move too quickly to improve instructional practices. The amount of time a teacher requires to make significant and lasting change depends on the nature of the challenge. For example, coaching to fine tune the questions a teacher asks students during conferring will probably take less time than supporting a teacher moving from teacher-centered to student-centered learning. The context determines the amount of time the teacher and coach collaborate.

Effective coaches allow teachers' needs and level of prior knowledge to set the pace of the coaching and learning. Coaches and teachers plan, debrief lessons, converse about professional articles, watch videos together, and pull out takeaways related to their collaboration.

EFFECTIVE COACHES ARE CURIOUS AND ASK QUESTIONS-OF THEMSELVES AND THE TEACHERS THEY COACH.

If the goal is to help teachers absorb and apply new ideas, coaching to change instructional practices or a class management style will require time. However, it's time well spent because, unlike quick fixes and solutions, teachers will bank enough practice and adequately enlarge their background knowledge to effect a lasting change.

However, before coaches can support teachers in these changes, they must first take time to build a trusting relationship. This can be done through observations, conversations, and negotiating a coaching agenda; consider our following suggestions to build trust before developing a formal coaching relationship with a teacher.

- **Extend an invitation** to a grade-level team or department explaining that it's okay if everyone doesn't immediately accept. Teachers who accept the invitation are eager to learn and grow. If those teachers are eager about working with a coach, their enthusiasm can spread and influence others to ask to join. However, forcing a teacher to accept a coaching invitation can have negative consequences. Dissatisfaction and anger spread quickly and can diminish the upbeat outlook of teachers who volunteered. To move more teachers to accept coaching, some administrators I've worked with set a reasonable time limit for one or more teachers to learn with a coach. Often, fear of changing prevents teachers from jumping on board. Time to talk to colleagues about how positive the coaching and learning relationship is can change negative perceptions. Ultimately, effective leaders will do everything they can to foster change through inviting, modeling, and providing professional learning opportunities.
- **Observe** by being integrally involved in a lesson. Spend one or two classes working with the teacher so students are comfortable with you supporting them.
- **Follow-up** after each observation with an email or handwritten note celebrating the positive aspects you noticed. Frame any needs you observed as questions for the teacher to consider.
- **Negotiate a plan** with the teacher to set the coaching agenda, create instructional plans, and schedule one-on-one meetings and collaborate in classes. Both the teacher and you have input into decisions. Let the teacher lead in setting priorities. If needed, you can raise questions to move the teacher's thinking to a different place.
- **Debrief** after collaborating on a lesson or observing the teacher facilitating a lesson. To have maximum impact, debriefing should occur on the day of the observation or the next day. The goal is for teachers to become self-evaluative and monitor

their teaching and students' learning by daily posing these questions to evaluate outcomes:

- What were students learning, and how do I know they learned it?
- What requires extra reflection and discussion?

Just as it's impossible to force students to read, it's equally impossible to force teachers to change. They need to see the relevance of changing and ultimately develop the mindset enabling them to work hard, learn, collaborate, and take necessary steps to transform their instructional practices and beliefs about how their students learn. When I extended a written invitation to fifth-grade teachers at Daniel Morgan Intermediate School to develop a student-centered approach to reading, three teachers volunteered. Their thoughts on coaching as a support for instructional changes are below.

REFLECTIONS ON BEING COACHED
An Interlude by Wanda Waters, Bridget Wilson,
and Stacey Yost

During our combined eighty years of teaching experience, we have attended and participated in numerous conferences, professional development trainings, best practice research, professional readings, and personal learning networks (PLNs). However, none of these has impacted our teaching and our students' learning as much as our empowering year-long coaching experience with Laura Robb.

From the beginning, Laura made it abundantly clear through her actions and words that she would be working *beside us* as a teacher. We would be a team; she was the coach, and we were her colleagues. We had a shared goal to provide students with meaningful, effective reading instruction and grow readers by giving them voice, choice, and volume in their reading. We met frequently to ask questions, share struggles, and celebrate successes. Like all good coaches, Laura validated our concerns, working with us to find possible solutions.

When Laura assumed the role of teacher, she modeled explicit reading instruction as we took on the role of students. A debriefing always followed these lessons. Through this coaching strategy, we gained deeper understanding of the learning through the eyes of students. Afterward, we became the teacher and practiced the strategies Laura had modeled for us. This was not always easy. Initially, we were anxious to do what she was asking—a feeling shared by many of the students we teach. She provided positive feedback and suggestions to help us improve our craft. Through struggling, rethinking, and adjusting lessons, we eventually found successes.

Laura encouraged us to take risks and constantly reminded us it was okay to fail. We learned from our mistakes and became better teachers. Even when we struggled, she focused on our strengths and coached us with suggestions to help us grow. At no time did Laura claim to have all the answers; instead, she presented us with guiding questions to help us discover possible solutions. She validated our feelings, experiences, and frustrations, often by saying, "It's okay to slow down," and, "The next time will be better." These words were comforting and reminded us that our students' learning is a marathon—not a sprint.

As our coach, Laura encouraged us to take a hard look at our past classroom structure and teaching methods and identify where change was needed. Change was challenging even when we knew it was necessary. We strongly believed in the needed changes; however, we felt nervous and afraid. Laura planted in us the thought-provoking seed to make instructional decisions based on being responsive to our students' needs. While we nervously had to hand over control to our students and allow their needs to drive our instruction, she created a nonjudgmental environment in which we could be honest and reflective with ourselves and with each other as we transitioned from teacher-centered to student-centered classrooms.

We now found ourselves teaching in a relevant way, effective for our students. This had been our missing link. Our classrooms were filled with new, beautiful books at levels accessible to all our readers, and our students were given voice and choice in what they read. They used these books—in place of worksheets—to practice their reading skills and strategies. What a breath of fresh air! We found ourselves standing back and taking in the sight of students reading, talking about, and enjoying books *they* chose. In the past, our students had read four class novels a year. They now read a multitude of books of all genres and can practice reading skills as they read books they choose.

Having Laura in our classroom with us was an empowering and inspiring experience. As a coach, she experienced firsthand what we face daily. She earned our trust and respect by willingly joining our classrooms, and she created an atmosphere that made us feel safe and willing to take risks. Finally, she encouraged us to continue to enhance and strengthen our craft by being active on Twitter, reading professional publications, attending conferences, and sharing our experiences with colleagues.

As Laura demonstrated, effective coaching includes not only the coach modeling instructional strategies but also the "team members" practicing them throughout the year, problem-solving, and discussing what is happening in their classrooms. Additionally, investing the time needed to build trust between the coach and the teachers will make for a successful coaching experience positively impacting teachers and students.

QUALITIES OF A COACH

Whether I'm hiring a full-time person or considering asking a teacher to become a half-time coach, I (Evan) look for specific qualities. Sometimes identifying these qualities is easier in a teacher who works at your school, but with probing questioning techniques, you also can discover whether a potential new hire has them as well. Consider the following qualities and related questions to ask potential hires when seeking a new coach:

Growth mindset and self-efficacy are essential beliefs of a coach who knows a teacher's hard work and persistence, combined with the coach's support, can build positive relationships and effect meaningful change. In addition, believing in Carol Dweck's power of "yet" can change a teacher's instruction and students' learning.
- Why are growth mindset, the power of "yet," and self-efficacy crucial to effective coaching?
- Can you give an example of changing your personal mindset and an example of helping a teacher or student change his or hers?

Instructional expertise in literacy or specific content subjects is essential for coaches to move teachers forward.

- Can you share a teaching or coaching experience demonstrating how your instructional expertise affected planning, implementation, and assessment?

Ongoing learning, reading professional articles and books to build background knowledge, and recommending materials to teachers is imperative.

- Can you name and discuss a recent professional book or article you read and explain how it affected your thinking and practice?

Being a keen observer who notices and shares what's working well and builds on the teacher's strengths is essential.

- Why is it important to use strengths to create instructional growth? Can you share an example?

Active listening allows the coach to respond effectively to what the teacher is saying.

- Why is it important for a coach to develop discussion points by observing and listening to a teacher? Share an example.

Flexibility allows coaches to follow the teacher's lead through frequent conversations. Coaches should avoid fixed, premade agendas or goals, allowing teachers to inform the goals you work on just as students inform the practice and interventions teachers offer them.

- How does flexibility contribute to being a successful coach?
- Describe a time you needed to be flexible and explain how you found a successful outcome.

Pointing out progress and celebrating successes is essential to encouraging teacher growth. Coaches who have a growth mindset and self-efficacy are more apt to point out and celebrate the growth they observe.

- How does your mindset contribute to helping others improve, and how does it help you improve?
- What indicators do you look for to gauge success, and why did you choose these indicators?

Schools without coaches miss out on opportunities to help teachers grow into more reflective, skilled, and intentional practitioners. Effective coaches support school-wide initiatives and, through their coaching, prepare students for their futures. They listen to teachers to understand issues and engage in conversations to help teachers change their practices, mindsets, teaching narratives, and self-efficacy. A coach committed to teacher growth—and a teacher wanting to improve—can change the way students learn and interact with each other and the teacher, resulting in a positive and trusting learning community.

REFLECT! DISCUSS WITH COLLEAGUES! REVISIT!

- Considering your school's instructional challenges, how can coaches act as key components of positive change?
- What are the first steps you need to consider when bringing instructional coaching to your building?

—— **Share your thoughts and ideas! #teammakers** ——

CHAPTER 9
COLLABORATION AND RELATIONSHIPS MATTER

If members of a school district cultivate collaboration and trusting relationships, then three qualities can develop among administrators and staff: self-efficacy, empathy, and mindsets open to new ideas. In these districts, school leaders are TeamMakers who work to nurture these three qualities among students—qualities needed for college, career, and a productive life.

When I (Laura) started teaching more than forty years ago, teachers worked alone. They rarely communicated with one another, and many openly expressed that teaching was a lonely life. Feelings of isolation extended to students as well, who in those days sat in rows, worked independently, and could only volunteer to answer teacher-posed questions during recitation.

Several years ago, when I spent a year learning with high school teachers in Virginia, the principal and I shared the goal of wanting students to learn in teams, have conversations and plan presentations together, and listen to and value diverse perspectives. Even though their students sat in rows, when I made my twice-a-month visits to the school, the teachers and I learned together in collaborative groups, part of the workshop approach the principal and I wanted them to bring to their classes. Equally important, the principal created opportunities during department meetings for his staff to engage in conversations about the learning they were doing with me.

Halfway through the school year, Mrs. Roberts, a ninth-grade English teacher, and I planned a collaborative lesson. Before her students arrived, we moved their chairs into groups of four so each could easily converse about a different Langston Hughes poem, discuss the emotions their poem raised, and discover and share one big idea. As the students filed into class, one by one they moved their chairs back into rows and sat down. When I asked them why they had moved the chairs back into rows, they quickly answered, "That's the way we sit in here and other classes."

I suggested we try a different way of learning and promised to reserve time for them to evaluate their experience. They looked to Mrs. Roberts for approval, and, once she nodded, they returned the chairs to teams. Some expressed initial distrust of the change, but reading and discussing the poem helped them suspend this feeling. Mrs. Roberts and I circulated among groups, affirming their active listening and respect for diverse ideas. Our positive comments injected energy into their conversations. Approximately five minutes before the class ended, I invited students to jot their reactions to the lesson on a piece of notebook paper. All agreed that hearing classmates' ideas highlighted different ways of reacting to the poem. A few felt good to be in a group and not sitting and working alone. It was a solid beginning, but students needed more experiences to feel confident about exchanging ideas and risking an interpretation different from their peers' view.

After Mrs. Roberts shared her lessons at an English department meeting, another teacher invited me to help her plan a series of collaborative lessons around short stories. The collaborative learning teachers were doing with me, combined with these two teachers sharing instructional changes they were making in their classes, along with the principal's open support of collaboration in flexible groups, led to all English teachers taking the plunge into collaboration by the end of the school year.

Several weeks of students learning and discussing in groups passed before teachers and I observed students trusting each other enough to share different ideas—trusting that no one would ridicule their thinking, trusting that politely disagreeing was okay, and trusting that friendships and relationships wouldn't derail because of a comment or observation. It took a full year for the former culture of separation and completing work alone to transform into a culture of collaboration, with students discussing together, sharing written ideas, valuing diverse interpretations of texts, and learning in flexible groups. Most teachers recognized that the initiative had to continue the next school year.

Flexible seating alone wasn't responsible for the transformation. It simply served as a catalyst for the instructional changes modeled by teachers—changes they had practiced during our workshop sessions. It took two years for literary discussions, writing about reading in readers' notebooks, and using writing to develop analytical paragraphs and essays to completely replace worksheet packets and writing prompts for essays.

Although change can eventually come over time, for change to transform traditional practices into a collaborative class culture, it's beneficial for teachers to learn in flexible groups. By discussing professional materials, they enhance their understanding of the instructional changes they will bring to students. While teachers learn together, collaboration and small-group discussions become part of their model. At this point, teachers gain the experience and background knowledge needed to bring what they are learning to their students.

COLLABORATION: A SKILL FOR STUDENTS' FUTURE

Educators see collaboration as a creative problem-solving skill based on the principle that pooling the expertise and creativity of many minds far exceeds what one mind working alone can accomplish. Effective collaboration has always been an important skill, but for the last one hundred years, it has not usually been integrated into students' learning. For students to compete in the workplace, however, they need collaborative experiences to develop their ability to think creatively, analyze materials, and solve challenging problems.

Stanford and Boston University conducted studies on the benefits of collaboration in modern workplaces. The results make a compelling case for collaboration over working alone, showing that working in a team:

- Motivated members to readily take on challenges
- Resulted in members sticking to their task 64 percent longer than those working alone
- Enabled groups to be five times as likely to be high performing than individuals working alone

We have observed entire school districts—from the superintendent to school administrators, to teachers, and sometimes to parents—collaborate on learning initiatives and improve communication. Superintendents set the tone for school principals. If they champion collaboration among district staff as a learning and problem-solving tool, most likely principals will advocate for collaboration in their schools. This modeled commitment to collaboration can trickle down to the classroom level, where students' learning can be positively impacted.

Collaboration was not part of my (Evan's) early teaching experiences. My supervisor met me in my classroom a few days before I started my first teaching position as a seventh-grade history teacher and plunked down on my desk an annotated textbook and a set of worksheets for students. "This is all you'll need," she said. "I usually finish the first seventeen units by May. If you get close to that, you'll have a good year." (I can still recall my feelings of anxiety rising as she spoke.)

"I have some questions," I told her.

"I'm off to a meeting; don't have time. You'll be fine. Just push them [students]." This was my first and only interaction about instruction; it was a sink-or-swim environment.

A friend of mine from a neighboring school district had a similar experience. She told me about her principal—a top-down decision maker whose leadership style affected the style of other administrators, department heads, and team leaders. The principal delivered school policies and rules, expecting everyone to fall in line and follow. This leadership was counterproductive to my friend's efforts to create a collaborative school and ultimately led her to leave and find a school right for her.

To foster collaboration in schools, principals must step aside, view leadership through a different lens, and recognize that collaboration can be a positive force. We have identified seven positive effects collaboration can have on schools' staffs and students. Collaboration:

- Creates higher teacher commitment to school initiatives because administrators value teachers' thoughts and suggestions
- Fosters teacher responsibility to students' learning as they work in teams to solve problems
- Builds trust among staff and administrators as they work together and get to know one another

- Encourages innovative thinking to develop new and useful ideas
- Provides a model for students' learning and benefits students, making teachers more likely to use it
- Improves instruction when teachers set aside time to discuss practices and students' needs
- Supports strong parent–community ties through work with parent and local community groups, thereby broadening the supportive network for children and staff

Collaborative opportunities also enable administrators, staff, and students to get to know one another and develop trusting relationships.

RELATIONSHIPS MATTER!

We believe students don't learn from teachers they dislike or teachers they perceive dislike them. And it doesn't matter whether these negative feelings can be justified or if they are solely students' perceptions. For the children, the feelings are real.

My (Laura) fifth-grade year created unfortunate memories I still recall. I believed my teacher disliked me the moment I set foot in her class. My brother had given her a hard time, and she assumed I would follow in his footsteps. I was compliant and quiet and tried to complete daily worksheets, but her mind was made up. I believed she felt my brother's persona would take over my personality one day, and she would happily punish me.

One morning she asked me to stand in front of the room and told my classmates to look at my overly large feet, referring to them as "canal boats." I wanted to shrink my feet! I would have done anything to reduce them from size ten to six. My peers were silent; their eyes revealed how sad and frightened they were for me. After what felt like an eternity, she sent me back to my seat. Believe me, she spared no one; her talent for spotting a weakness humiliated many of my classmates. Parent complaints did little to change the situation, as she had been teaching for more than thirty years in the school, and surviving her class had become a rite of passage for ten-year-old students.

Fifth grade was my worst school year ever. What I did and learned is a blur. My teacher's legacy for me was making me self-conscious about my shoe size for many years. Clearly, this teacher didn't try to cultivate trusting relationships with her students, and many suffered emotionally and academically because of her.

Teachers who put children first and continually work to nurture positive connections with each student understand that trusting relationships positively affect how children learn, listen, and interact with their teacher and peers. Because learning is social and children learn from each other as well as from their teacher, the class environment matters. Setting the right tone starts at the top. Again, the way the superintendent treats and relates to school administrators impacts relationship building between school administrators and staff and trickles down to the interactions between teachers and students. Trusting relationships between administrators and teachers—and between teachers and students—can:

- Empower all groups to take risks and be daring
- Improve efficacy and growth mindset
- Increase purposeful risk-taking
- Nurture a positive school climate and culture
- Support students' learning
- Increase collaboration and communication
- Build effective social skills
- Motivate staff and students to do their best
- Build a school-wide community of learners

Relationship building starts the first day teachers and students enter their classroom, and the trust it produces can inspire students to

TEACHERS WHO PUT CHILDREN FIRST AND CONTINUALLY WORK TO NURTURE POSITIVE CONNECTIONS WITH EACH STUDENT UNDERSTAND THAT TRUSTING RELATIONSHIPS POSITIVELY AFFECT HOW CHILDREN LEARN, LISTEN, AND INTERACT WITH THEIR TEACHER AND PEERS.

work hard and develop positive relationships with their peers. Administrators also play an important role in relationship building, as assistant superintendent Dr. Kris Felicello explains:

RELATIONSHIP BUILDING
An Interlude by Kris Felicello, EdD

Building-level administrators face more challenges than ever before, and to be as effective as they can, they need support from the central office. As an assistant superintendent, I must not forget the challenges of being in the trenches everyday—as a classroom teacher or the leader of the building. To ensure that I remain sensitive to them, at the start and end of every day, I reflect on questions to help me continually build trusting, positive relationships among all members of my district. I frequently revisit three questions:

- How can I stay connected, be visible, and build the trusting relationships necessary for effective leadership?
- How can I support my principals?
- How can I help other administrators recognize the importance of relationship building?

My success in this position is based on providing opportunities to develop leadership skills in all district personnel regardless of their title. I must put the needs of those I lead ahead of my own. I want to inspire and reinvigorate a community of open-minded learners and leaders who work to develop our youth into healthy, happy, curious, intelligent people who will make our society a better place. But the first step toward achieving these goals is to build important relationships with district personnel. I've discovered that this can be done in a variety of ways:

Get your hands dirty. Be visible in the schools in your district. Set up your office, and work out of one school for a day. Be available, but do your best not to get in the way. Attend important meetings at schools as much as possible. Observe the happenings of the schools, and note the challenges and causes of stress. Be willing to pitch in when you observe a need: cover a class for a teacher or help with lunch duty.

Give permission. The realization that teaching all of the standards New York expects teachers to cover is impossible encouraged me to give permission to faculty to teach using their own unique talents, always keeping in mind that teaching is an art and each child's needs are unique. Be courageous and creative in finding opportunities to give permission to teachers.

Build relationships. Notice what can be celebrated about your colleagues. Know what they are passionate about, and get to know their families. Pay attention to what they do and say, and affirm what's working well. Say something positive to another administrator, teacher, or student, or email something you noticed to make the positive connection so important in building trusting relationships.

A few years ago, my boss taught me a lesson, clarifying the importance of prioritizing people. I was frantically working in my office, diligently checking items off my endless to-do list, when my superintendent walked in and said, "Kris, it's time to go." Frankly, I felt annoyed that the superintendent insisted I interrupt my overloaded day to attend a funeral of the parent of a teacher I barely knew. My frustration only increased during the car ride to the church.

When we walked into the church, the teacher spotted us. Immediately, his eyes brimmed with tears, and he embraced my boss in a hug seeming to last for days. In between tears, he said again and again, "I can't believe you guys came." The superintendent patted his back and whispered in her soft, motherly voice, "Of course we came."

This moment continues to be imprinted in my mind, forcing me to confront my own priorities and ask, "What is more important—completing tasks at work or providing support and compassion to a teacher?" Attending this funeral service changed my values and enabled me to recognize that my decisions should always be about prioritizing and nurturing people and sending the message, "I care and will be there for you!"

Take risks. The most effective leaders encourage teachers, principals, aides, and even lunch monitors to take risks and try different ways of teaching and collaborating. Whether supporting them to try a new learning technique, topic, platform, or system, or attend a conference, when we empower people to follow their passions, magic can happen. People learn, share ideas, and interact, resulting in improved instruction and attitudes. School cultures shift to become more positive as teacher leaders develop; trusting relationships among all stakeholders grow; and instruction becomes student-focused, reaching and engaging every child.

The best central office leaders know that just because they have the title, they do not have a monopoly on ideas. The primary purpose of a central office administrator is to remove the barriers teachers may face or feel by cultivating positive and lasting relationships and tapping into the ideas and expertise of all staff. Remember, relationships among stakeholders in a district make each school a better place for kids.

INCREASE STUDENTS' LEARNING

When I (Evan) was in elementary and middle school, relationship building wasn't on most teachers' radar. On the first day of school, my teachers dove into academic work and gave a hefty amount of homework. They didn't know much about me; I was simply a grade in their gradebook based on classwork, homework, and tests. Such a culture diminishes the importance of relationships and reduces schooling to academics and covering the curriculum. It ignores the social nature of learning and the fact students with diverse experiences, background knowledge, and needs arrive at school every day hopeful to learn.

It's important for children to learn and enjoy the process of learning. Trusting relationships with teachers, other staff, and administrators increase the likelihood for learning. When we think of Maslow's work, we remember that feeling safe and having basic needs met is truly important. We're also reminded of an old saying: "You can't do Bloom's Taxonomy until you take care of the basic Maslow needs." When administrators and teachers have high expectations and treat one another and students with kindness and empathy, the environment is ripe for self-efficacy and a growth mindset to flourish—ingredients needed to bring a student-centered approach into schools. And students develop a lifelong skill: building and nurturing trusting relationships in personal and professional lives!

REFLECT! DISCUSS WITH COLLEAGUES! REVISIT!

- How can collaboration throughout a district change each school's culture?
- How do trusting relationships affect collaboration and learning?

—— **Share your thoughts and ideas! #teammakers** ——

CHAPTER 10
FROM TEACHER-CENTERED TO STUDENT-CENTERED LEARNING

———

When I (Evan) learned I was to become principal of Johnson Williams Middle School, I spent a day with a friend who was completing his first year as a middle school principal in West Virginia. My friend told me his goal was to start changing his teaching and learning culture the following year. He had devoted his first year to building relationships with teachers and discussing change with grade-level teams—a point I tucked into my memory.

My friend and I visited several classes, and I observed that students sat in rows in most classes, spoke only when asked a question, completed stacks of worksheets, and listened to lectures or did round robin reading. These may seem like outdated classroom practices, but they still exist. Certainly it is time for schools to change.

My visit reminded me of a story another principal colleague shared that still resonates with me. He was coaching a seventh-grade English teacher, Anna, hoping to help her develop more empathy and compassion for her students. A thirty-year veteran, Anna used the same curriculum, books, and worksheets every year, and she never strayed from her original lesson plans. Anna's curriculum required students to memorize poetry; however, they were unnerved when they had to perform the poems because Anna took off points if they missed or changed words. Students sat in rows, and Anna's comments about their work or behavior were often sarcastic. As a result, her students learned they had to be passive and compliant to do well in her fact-driven classroom.

Perhaps this teaching model prepared students years ago to work in factories or on farms—but it won't prepare students for the future. Best practice and research show that many of Anna's practices were inappropriate. So why do some of these practices still exist? Most likely, teachers like Anna draw on their own education memories and bring similar experiences to their students. To facilitate change in some of Anna's practices, my friend observed her teaching and followed up with conversations, inviting her to reflect on her students' feelings. He also gave Anna professional articles to read, discussed these with her, and steered her toward building positive relationships and allowing students to discuss their reading. He celebrated every small increment of change he noticed with a note or email.

With these stories in mind, I began my position at Johnson Williams with three personal focus areas: observation, seeking to understand, and conversation. Teacher-centered and teacher-controlled classrooms were the rule at my school, but, fortunately, not because of a spirit to defy best practice. This was simply what some thought was best; it was what they had always done. While there were pockets of excellence, including a more student-centered approach to learning, I knew widespread change would take time. I also understood, for teachers to embrace student-centered learning, they needed to develop a mental model of what it looked like as well as understand its benefits to their students and themselves.

I needed to help staff learn new ways of organizing a classroom and teaching. I asked teachers to read professional articles on the benefits of student-centered learning and invited them to ask questions and comment on the information when we discussed these during faculty meetings. I encouraged pairs of teachers to observe a student-centered approach in other schools so they could discuss their experience together. Building and reshaping their background knowledge, I believed, could change their teaching narratives. Be aware that doing this takes time and patience, but it is the only way to impact substantive change. Not every teacher will change, but given the time to learn and process, many will. Of course, another way to incorporate student-centered leaning into your school's culture is to hire new teachers who believe in and have used this approach when other teachers retire or leave.

To clearly see the differences between teacher-centered and student-centered learning, review the following chart comparing the two.

TEACHER-CENTERED LEARNING	STUDENT-CENTERED LEARNING
Orderly, quiet classroom as students work alone.	Lots of talk and discussions as students communicate and collaborate with a partner or small group.
Teacher controls when students talk and what they do and learn. Learning is passive.	Students use inquiry to drive their learning and practice communicative and collaborative skills through group work. Teacher and students share learning. Learning is active.
Whole-class instruction is the rule.	Whole-class instruction as well as small group instruction, and targeted intervention and enrichment of individuals and groups, are the rule.
Covering curriculum drives the pace of classes.	Students' needs drive the pace of the class. Responding to students' needs requires adjusting curriculum and reteaching so all students learn.
Teacher directs learning. Students have no choices.	Students practice directing their learning through inquiry, discussions, collaborative problem-solving, and critical thinking to effectively complete tasks.
Teacher creates rules for behavior and due dates for work.	Students suggest behavior expectations for diverse learning situations and negotiate work deadlines with the teacher.

TEACHER-CENTERED LEARNING	STUDENT-CENTERED LEARNING
Students read the same materials and complete the same tasks (often worksheets).	Differentiation enables students to use materials they can read and learn from and complete authentic tasks.
Long lectures and copying notes from the board are part of teacher-centered instruction. Students have difficulty listening and concentrating.	Students do the learning and are actively involved with reading, note-taking, and writing about reading.
Students sit in rows.	Seating is flexible and can change as the kinds of learning experiences change.
Students complete one-size-fits-all tasks.	Students are involved in innovative learning such as genius hour and project-based learning.

Negotiation is an important part of student-centered learning. With their teacher, students can negotiate behavior expectations, deadline dates for work, room arrangements, and diverse ways to showcase their learning. Only in an active-learning classroom do teachers provide students with multiple opportunities to do the following:

- *Improve communication*, including active listening and using words to express ideas.
- *Develop empathy* for others as they collaborate and read books about diverse cultures and religions.
- *Become passionate* about learning because they have choice and are interacting with peers.
- *Use inquiry* to drive learning and foster curiosity
- *Practice flexibility* by collaborating and planning projects, discussing materials, and adjusting plans, researching, and developing and sharing tasks.
- *Hone critical thinking* as they discuss, analyze texts and videos, and transfer learning to different situations with a partner or small group.

- *Persevere* when challenges feel insurmountable because groups support members and empower them to continue to work hard.

When students have choices, actively do the learning, work in teams, and confer with teachers and peers, they develop the skills needed for success, whether they continue their education or apply for a job. In the following interlude, eleventh-grader Joe O'Such discusses why he favors a student-centered approach:

STUDENT-CENTERED LEARNING
An Interlude by Joe O'Such

With classroom paradigms and pedagogy constantly shifting and updating, student-centered learning has become a heavily discussed topic within the teaching profession. And it should be. Much like the customer being a focal point in any successful business, students are the "customers" of education and need to be the focus of schools. Student-centered learning keeps the focus on students and appeals to them in part because it tends to create a more engaging environment.

I attend the Academy of Science in Loudoun County, Virginia, a powerful example of student-centered learning, which employs this concept in several aspects of its classes. The math classes fully embrace the concept, with students typically leading discussions on homework and classwork problems, with the teacher's wealth of knowledge available to support and show the thought process behind a problem. All students are assigned a problem to present and explain. The teacher also may ask stimulating questions about future evolutions of the problem or the application.

The science classes offer labs and succeeding discussions, which are also student led with the teacher again on standby. Students will sometimes lead a review of homework or other assignments, and student questions are periodically redirected to the class, creating a powerful tool in which students learn from each other. The teacher operates with flexibility and can modify the curriculum on the fly, based on classroom real-time discussions and feedback.

In student-centered learning, students play a critical part in their education and assessments. Teachers should never be afraid to ask their students for input. Student feedback is immensely important and should be taken with the utmost seriousness. As a business takes customer feedback to better their product, a teacher should take student feedback to elevate their pedagogy. Although some will make ridiculous suggestions, most will be sincere and thoughtful. Students also will listen to their peers, sometimes more so than to teachers. By having students answer student questions, not only is the answer sometimes given in a more simplified manner but students are also furthering their own knowledge and speaking abilities by personally explaining a concept.

Student-centered learning is crucial for future excellence in education. By preparing students to collaborate to solve problems and providing them with an active-learning education, they will be prepared to tackle future problems.

THOUGHTS ON CHANGE

How can teachers move to a student-centered approach to teaching and learning? What drives this change? These are questions we discuss often. However, expecting change to happen quickly simply because the desire exists invites teachers to reverse their present practices without building a firm foundation of knowledge and understanding. The passion, dream, and goal might be in place, but the mental model is hazy or has missing parts. To minimize the potential frustration and anxiety of change and to help teachers make an imaginative leap to a new teaching style, principals need to create a safe environment to encourage taking risks, asking questions, and learning. When principals recognize that teachers need to form a solid picture of where the change can go, they can support them by fortifying them with information.

TEN CONDITIONS SUPPORTING TEACHER CHANGE

To aid principals in their effort to support teachers through change, we recommend the following conditions. These can enable staff to embrace shifts in teaching and learning to create a student-centered approach.

1. **Pinpoint needs.** Through collaboration and conversation, identify a need and build support among staff.

2. **Get everyone on the team.** Work to build consensus among staff through conversations with teams and departments, but also realize that seeking 100 percent agreement on initiatives is counterproductive.

3. **Build background knowledge.** When most of the staff is in favor of the change, share change-focused reading materials and invite team leaders, department heads, and the librarian to offer professional articles that staff can study and discuss. Sharing these electronically allows everyone to comment and raise questions.

4. **Simulate instructional changes.** Organize teachers into groups and engage them in new teaching practices using professional articles. Full faculty meetings are the ideal place for this. Invite teachers to learn this way several times during the year, emulating the same creativity and learning styles found in dynamic classrooms.

5. **Extend learning.** Suggest that teachers watch videos on a topic to create a mental model of this approach. Offer these during team or department meetings so teachers can share their feelings, reactions, and understandings, and discuss how the information might transfer to their classes.

6. **Reach parents.** Use technology to build parents' support about change. The principal, teachers, and librarian can post videos, podcasts, and newsletters on the school's website or use other social media platforms.

7. **Extend an invitation.** Invite teachers wanting to implement change in their classes to meet with like-minded colleagues and discuss first steps. We always encourage organic bottom-up change, although the principal and literacy coach should attend this meeting. Not all teachers will rush to volunteer. Some may not feel ready, and others may wait to observe results and the reactions from administrators. This is fine; starting small is beneficial because it's easier to offer feedback to a small group.

8. **Encourage peer partnerships.** Recommend that teachers invested in change partner up to discuss successes and needs and to observe one another.

9. **Have sharing conversations.** At team or department meetings, invite teachers to discuss how they feel about instructional initiatives and how they affect students' learning. Invite them to share mini-lessons and students' responses. Such conversations reveal the benefits of changes and can instill the courage to move forward in teachers who haven't made a commitment yet.

10. **Develop a positive culture.** Advocating positivity is a choice. Urge all teachers to embrace goals and research-based instructional changes, understanding that a few will resist and refuse to change. In this case, try one of two strategies: (1) Negotiate with resistant teachers to establish a time limit for them to implement changes and provide them with extra support to build their self-confidence to take risks; or (2) Replace retired and departed staff with teachers who are enthusiastic about school goals and have the experience and background knowledge to implement them. Change can be difficult, but teachers choosing to resist it when the choice hurts students challenge a principal's leadership and beliefs and what the principal is willing to tolerate.

We recommend teachers start small and work with a colleague for support. Together, decide on one change within your comfort zone, and practice it until you and your students are comfortable doing something new. Then add another change. Consider reading *Shift This: How to Implement Gradual Changes for MASSIVE Impact in Your Classroom*, by Joy Kirr (2017). It's an excellent guide to making incremental changes to a student-centered approach.

START SMALL AND WORK WITH A COLLEAGUE FOR SUPPORT.

One-size-fits-all learning stifles curiosity; students check at the classroom door their desire to question and be creative. In 1985, Gordon Wells wrote a groundbreaking book, *The Meaning Makers*. He pointed out that we learn through stories and described learning at school as "the guided reinvention of knowledge." The teacher's responsibility is to create hands-on learning experiences so students actively "do" to build an extensive knowledge base supporting critical and creative thinking.

We invite you to develop a relationship with the young child deep inside you. Harvest the curiosity, creativity, and risk-taking natural to your learning before you entered school. Dream new stories about teaching and learning. Move away from lecture and copying notes, and invite students to work in teams and use inquiry. Look closely at students' writing and interactions, and listen carefully to their talk and questions to gather information to make instructional decisions to support each student. Individualized help is beneficial to students because it strengthens their self-confidence and self-efficacy, aiding them to learn and progress in all subjects. Through this they continually refine their ability to collaborate, communicate, analyze, and problem-solve—tools they will need to meet the uncertainties of the future.

REFLECT! DISCUSS WITH COLLEAGUES! REVISIT!

- Why is a student-centered approach to learning important for today's students?
- What is needed for you to make the shift to inquiry-based and student-focused learning?

—— **Share your thoughts and ideas! #teammakers** ——

PART IV
Changing Mindsets through Professional Learning

Ongoing professional learning is essential to developing district-wide change. Evan and I don't intend to make more work for teachers and administrators. Instead, we offer practical suggestions for learning within the school day, during flipped faculty meetings and team and department meetings. Here's the caveat: we recommend that teachers learn in ways they will teach their students, firmly believing that by experiencing collaboration, student-led discussions, choice, project-based learning, etc., teachers will be prepared to bring these practices to their students.

We invite teachers and administrators to adopt self-directed learning by joining Twitter, Facebook, and other social media platforms. If we empower educators to keep abreast of best practice research, we can fulfill our vision of district-wide teams who have the expertise and experience to understand and advance change in schools that enable everyone to cope with a rapidly evolving world.

Finally, we place the spotlight on self-efficacy and collective efficacy and offer ways the principal can build and enlarge both. When teachers, administrators, and staff believe they can positively affect the progress and growth of students, collective efficacy exists in a school. Continually supporting the development of self-efficacy and collective efficacy is the knowledge teachers gather from professional learning. In addition to suggestions for cultivating collective efficacy, it's important to know that this belief can positively affect the learning and progress of all students, from developing to proficient learners. And that is a goal of *TeamMakers*!

CHAPTER 11
FLIPPING TRADITIONAL MEETINGS

———

During traditional faculty meetings, the principal relays important information to staff and, occasionally, invites them to share comments. Topics such as scheduling changes, sports events, guest speakers, behavior issues, fire drills, and parent conferences dominate meetings. Flipping these meetings to focus on substantive topics such as best practices, efficacy, growth mindset, grading systems, relationships, and integrating technology to enhance learning will ultimately benefit students and better prepare them for the future.

My (Laura) memories of faculty meetings can be summed up by two words: *boring* and *repetitive*. Meetings scheduled for one hour often ended after two hours. Teachers argued about everything—how to deal with dress code infractions, students who didn't complete homework or classwork, behavior issues, unreturned library books, and complaining parents. Every teacher wanted to be heard. The agenda rarely digressed from these topics, and most of us dreaded Monday afternoons. During my first year of teaching at this school, I noticed teachers brought knitting, crocheting, and mending to meetings. Men graded papers and grumbled about not being able to knit. I confess: I joined the women, and in one school year, knitted a sweater for my husband.

Today, when email connects schools and staff in districts, there's no excuse for these kinds of meetings. Much administrative information can be communicated in an email sent to staff two days before a department, team, or full faculty meeting. Scheduled meetings then can then be used for their ideal purpose: professional learning and generating ways to better support students.

PROFESSIONAL LEARNING MEETINGS

I (Evan) too have sat through faculty meetings in which topics could have been studied easily by committees and results communicated to staff in some other way. It makes no sense for principals to expect students to collaborate and problem solve and yet lead faculty meetings in which teachers passively receive information. Meetings are the ideal place for teachers to experience learning the way you hope students will learn in their classrooms. By emulating the learning experiences of great classrooms, you expose teachers to innovative types of learning and open conversations about how collaboration, communication, analytical and creative thinking, and choice can impact students' learning.

To help you begin the process of "flipping" your meetings, I recommend you set aside four faculty meetings for teachers to experience student-centered learning and connect what they learn to classroom practices. During these meetings, teachers will collaborate with each other, make choices about their learning, think critically, and apply what they are learning. Before the first meeting, select topics of study either aligning with school initiatives or drawn from instructional discussions with staff. First, find an article that aligns with your goals for each topic. As an example, type "articles about student-centered learning" into a search engine to locate articles about this topic.

FIRST FACULTY MEETING

- Organize faculty into groups of four to six, and introduce the available topics. Offer each group a choice of topic and provide the article related to their topic. Have groups read and then discuss their article.
- Each group chooses a spokesperson to share with the other groups what their group discussed. Invite a volunteer to record ideas on chart paper or a whiteboard.
- Ask groups to discuss ways they could create or incorporate student-focused learning experiences (or another topic) in their classes, and ask groups to share. Challenge staff to use what they have learned to bring more intentional change to

their classes, and encourage them to share at the second meeting how they do this.

SECOND FACULTY MEETING

- Read teachers' recorded ideas to recap what was discussed at the first meeting.
- Invite teachers to share a lesson demonstrating how they incorporated one of these ideas.
- Ask groups to read and discuss a different article, focusing on creativity and analytical thinking or any other area you and your staff want to work on, and invite staff to consider how they could integrate these ideas into their lessons.
- Groups choose a different spokesperson to share their ideas, and again record on the chart paper or whiteboard.
- Invite groups to discuss how to integrate these ideas into their teaching, and challenge them to try something they learned before the next faculty meeting.

THIRD FACULTY MEETING

- Recap what the group discussed at the second meeting by posting the teachers' recorded ideas.
- Invite teachers to share the ideas from the first and second meetings they integrated into their lessons.
- Invite groups to discuss (1) how they felt about getting to choose the articles they read and (2) how they can give students choice in their classes.

FOURTH FACULTY MEETING

- Recap what teachers discussed at the third meeting by posting the teachers' recorded ideas.
- Ask teachers to reflect on their experiences, discussions, and reading materials, and create a list of learning experiences they could integrate into their lessons.
- Ask groups to share their ideas, calling for a volunteer to record them.
- Ask each group to revisit, share, and discuss the ideas in their articles and how each impacts instruction and instructional changes.

How would this model change the typical dynamic of your past or present faculty meetings? If your school needs to flip meetings and focus on meaningful change, where is the best place to start? Change can be big or small, but if you do nothing to change, don't expect a different result. As you think about change, we encourage you to reflect on these additional questions:

- Are your actions creating an environment in which you encourage change?
- Are you communicating why there's a need for change without offending those who are happy with the way things are?
- In what ways are you celebrating and being a champion for those—inside and outside your school—who positively embrace impactful change?

Learning together is not a one-shot deal! That's why it's important to continually use flipped faculty meetings for professional learning. Instead of always leading professional study, invite pairs or groups of teachers to take the lead.

ACCEPT WHERE TEACHERS ARE

As you work to bring change and increase understanding of all team members, it is important to know that each staff member will have a different view of change. I (Evan) can usually place staff into one of three categories:

- Resistant to change
- Ambivalent about change
- Willing to enthusiastically embrace new ideas

Equally important is to reflect deeply on how you plan to bring staff together when they're divided this way. When you start an article or book study, consider what strategies you might use to bring each group along. You might meet with groups individually to hear their perspectives on change and offer them articles to read and then meet with them again to discuss articles and encourage them to be open to learning and changing.

Even after reading and discussing articles, however, teachers may not absorb all the key points. Their background knowledge, level of investment, and personal experiences will determine their understanding. Be positive. Notice small changes in teachers' attitudes, and offer positive feedback in emails or one-to-one conversations. When a strategy or learning experience is new to teachers, provide them with background knowledge and hands-on experiences they need to develop the depth of understanding to bring the strategy or experience to their students.

Below you'll find ten ways teachers at your school can foster and build collaborative learning experiences. Teachers will benefit by discussing these suggestions during meetings, always through the lens of how each one fits into their subject and instructional practices.

BE POSITIVE. NOTICE SMALL CHANGES IN TEACHERS' ATTITUDES, AND OFFER POSITIVE FEEDBACK IN EMAILS OR ONE-TO-ONE CONVERSATIONS.

Create collaborative learning spaces. Encourage teachers to abandon rows of desks separating and isolating students. For collaboration to take place and students to have opportunities to choose and discuss materials, they need to work together in groups or with partners who report back to the group. Merely shifting out of rows to groups does not change lecture; lecturing to students sitting in groups is no different than lecturing to rows. The key is for the seating in the class to mirror the instructional methods of the teacher. Only then have shifts in learning occurred.

Bring choice of reading materials to instructional texts. Invite school librarians to meet with teachers to explain how they can help teachers select books related to units or topics to meet the diverse instructional needs of students in their classes. Additional books offer students more reading choices and provide them with a wider range to support their understanding of topics, themes, and genre structure.

Initiate student-led discussions. Teachers can build on the "turn and talk" strategy, asking students to turn to their right or left and discuss a question about a read-aloud text or an aspect of a lesson. Next steps include asking students to discuss a text for five to fifteen minutes with a partner, using questions the pair composed. Students then transition to small-group discussions. Teachers needing background knowledge of student-led discussions will benefit from reading and discussing these books:

- Harvey Daniels, *Literature Circles: Voice and Choice in Book Clubs and Reading Groups*
- Laura Robb, *Read, Talk, Write: 35 Lessons That Teach Students to Analyze Fiction and Nonfiction*

Develop personalized learning. Through blended learning, technology, and inquiry, develop individual learning pathways for students. Invite them to work with you to set learning goals enabling you to help them move forward from where they are. Instead of one instructional method and one pacing guide for all, personalized learning allows you to adjust and customize the rate of learning for all students according to their strengths, needs, and interests.

Invite students to debrief. Ask students to discuss in class or on a class blog their reactions to student-led small group discussions of the short story they read:

- What worked and why?
- What can be improved and how?

This prompts students to problem solve using their creativity and communication skills.

Teach students to set goals. After they debrief a student-led discussion, groups and individuals can use the information gathered from the question, "What can be improved and how?" to set goals, consider their progress, and decide on next steps.

Integrate technology into all subjects. Use technology to enhance and transform how students learn. Technology can personalize learning, help students gain access to important information, enable students to communicate with others while working on a project, develop a blended learning environment, and provide specific support and practice. Because technology changes rapidly, the best way for the principal and staff to keep up is through professional learning. Principals should also encourage teachers to risk trying new technology with their students and then share their thoughts with their colleagues. The leader's responsibility is to create a culture in which innovation and intentional risk-taking are available to all staff.

Direct students to write about their reading. Research by Steve Graham, Karen Harris, and Tanya Santangelo (2015) indicates that when students write about books and other materials they can read, their comprehension can improve by twenty-four percentage points. This writing can be done across the curriculum and should be informal— on-the-spot reactions, connections, short summaries, and evaluations of information, characters' decisions, conflicts, and themes.

Use the jigsaw strategy. If you have several questions you want students to discuss, divide them among groups. Once groups discuss, they choose a spokesperson to explain their ideas to the class. Jigsaw advances the flow of a lesson forward.

Try chat centers. A spin-off of jigsaw strategies, chat centers get students out of their seats and moving around the room. Create chat centers by posting questions about literary elements, vocabulary, or content topics on five to seven sheets around the room. Assign each group to a chat center, asking them to discuss and present their findings to the class. By working together, students have to adjust and clarify their ideas to communicate clearly and effectively so that classmates understand their thinking.

This list is not exhaustive; hopefully, it's a catalyst for dreaming, sharing stories, and generating additional ideas to inspire educators to prepare students for their future. We encourage teachers to work closely with a colleague, choose a strategy or concept they'd like to implement, share ideas, observe one another's classes, debrief, and, when both are comfortable, try another one. We always invite teachers to start small and add new learning practices slowly to ensure success and maintain the desire to take risks, learn, and grow.

When I notice teachers making changes in teaching practices, I celebrate by composing and sending an upbeat email or handwritten note. Celebrating teachers when they take risks and apply to lessons what they practiced at faculty meetings develops self-efficacy and the confidence they need to continually improve their craft.

REFLECT! **DISCUSS WITH COLLEAGUES!** **REVISIT!**

- How can your faculty and administration collaborate to flip faculty meetings and learn together? Discuss three possible topics for flipped faculty meetings in your building.

- Identify any roadblocks to changing faculty meetings that your school faces. Generate ideas that can help you overcome most roadblocks.

—— Share your thoughts and ideas! #teammakers ——

CHAPTER 12
BUILDING-LEVEL PROFESSIONAL LEARNING

———

Educators should be engaged in ongoing professional learning if schools want to effectively prepare students to become future problem solvers. Schools wanting to positively impact the way students learn will provide many learning opportunities for their staff that can impact students' emotional and intellectual development.

When I (Evan) first started teaching, the "train the trainer" model was the en-vogue method of professional development. One teacher or resource person would attend a conference and later present what he or she learned to all the teachers at school. Unfortunately, this model contains many drawbacks. Teachers received information filtered through the background knowledge and lens of the "trainer." A second roadblock is that the trainer might not have the experience and background knowledge to process and present the information with fidelity. Moreover, the trainers often didn't have an opportunity to share the information until months after attending the conference, diminishing their level of recall. When considering the "train the trainer" model, consider these questions:

- Can others make needed adjustments in instruction from information filtered through the lens of one person?
- Does the cost savings of sending one person to a conference provide the intended purpose of helping teachers who didn't attend?

Another professional development practice many schools embrace is inviting a well-known guest speaker to work with staff. However, unless the presenter receives input from the principal and staff based on teachers' needs, and uses this to construct the training, the speaker won't reach everyone. I (Laura) have been in a situation like this. I had been asked by a school district in Maine to present an active-learning workshop on differentiating reading instruction to fourth- through eighth-grade ELA teachers. However, on the morning of my presentation, the assistant superintendent ushered me into the high school gymnasium packed with two hundred fifty prekindergarten to twelfth-grade teachers, saying she believed everyone could benefit from the workshop.

Even though I tried to make differentiation relevant to all subjects and grades, it was a struggle. This difficult experience showed me that my topic could never resonate with an entire district's staff. In fact, most teachers believed their time would have been better spent setting up their classrooms, and I agreed. Had I been given a choice, I

PROFESSIONAL LEARNING IS THE OPPOSITE OF STAFF DEVELOPMENT: THE RESPONSIBILITY FOR LEARNING RESTS WITH THE TEACHER—NOT THE FACILITATOR.

would not have come to present a narrowly focused workshop to all teachers. I would have chosen to work with a small group of teachers. Although motivational speeches can appeal to an entire prekindergarten to twelfth-grade staff, attempting to present to an entire staff a collaborative, active learning, content-specific workshop designed for a small group didn't work—and won't work. This type of training rarely engages everyone and is not a good use of a school's money.

On the other hand, if a school has the funds, hiring a long-term consultant *can* benefit all staff. He/she can have a positive impact on teachers' instruction as well as on students' learning. When principals are aware of teachers' needs and communicate these to the consultant, a productive relationship can form. In addition, when the principal and other school administrators participate with teachers in these types of workshops, they convey that professional learning is important for everyone. Long-term consultants have come to my (Evan) school monthly to present active-learning workshops related to school-wide initiatives such as differentiation. Each monthly workshop ended with a debriefing to encourage staff feedback and questions. Afterward, the consultant and I discussed his/her input and ideas for the next month. A week before each visit, the consultant and I discussed at length the progress I noticed among teachers related to the initiative and the next steps needed.

STAFF DEVELOPMENT VERSUS PROFESSIONAL LEARNING

When continual professional learning deeply involves teachers, they reflect on improving their teaching so every student can experience success and progress. The key is on *learning*. Often, training for teachers is referred to as "staff development," implying that the facilitator's job is to "develop" the staff. In this model, the purpose is to transmit information about specific topics such as note-taking, making inferences, or test preparation. We find that these presentations are often passive, delivered over a few hours from a PowerPoint or a podium. For teachers, the experience isn't active or ongoing, and they usually receive no follow-up from the presenter or someone at the school. This kind of "development" is exactly what we want schools to avoid.

We've experienced dozens of staff development days and have observed, when only one to two occur during a school year, that they rarely transform teachers' practice. In addition, the principal or assistant principal often don't attend. When administrators don't experience a presentation, they cannot easily understand the need for funding requests for materials or coaching support.

Professional learning is the opposite of staff development: the responsibility for learning rests with the teacher—*not* the facilitator. Professional learning implies educators are professionals who continually enlarge their theory of how children learn and keep up with research-based best practices. Learning is ongoing and self-directed. As such, districts should offer numerous opportunities for teachers to collaborate and grow, using a long-term consultant, building-level administrators, teacher advocates, webinars, and online courses.

LEARNING FROM STUDENTS
AND COLLEAGUES

Teachers learn every day by carefully watching and listening to their students, reading and reflecting on students' written work, and engaging in daily conversations with them. These interactions spark the need for additional learning for teachers to be better decision makers during the day and to develop helpful scaffolds and interventions.

The principal is the catalyst for professional learning at the building level and sets the tone for ongoing learning by joining staff as they learn. I (Evan) foster professional learning with my staff by actively participating with them in discussions of articles during team, department, and full faculty meetings and through online conversations. Similarly, the superintendent and central office administrators promote and champion a growth mindset by wholeheartedly supporting ongoing learning throughout their district.

I (Laura) consulted in a district in which the superintendent demonstrated how much he valued professional learning by allocating to individual schools funds to purchase books for book studies and hiring substitute teachers to cover classes so teachers could observe classes in a different district. Additionally, because this district was large, prohibiting the superintendent and other central office staff from attending personally, they decided to participate online in a different school once or twice per year, showing their support for ongoing professional learning and encouraging administrators and staffs to develop Professional Learning Networks (PLNs). By doing this, the superintendent communicated two messages to school administrators and staff:

- Professional learning and developing a PLN are important.
- All members of a school community, including central office staff, benefit from professional learning.

PROFESSIONAL LEARNING STARTS
WITH THE SUPERINTENDENT
An Interlude by Milton Ramirez, EdD

Many agree the superintendent is like the CEO of a school district, with responsibilities ranging from spending and finance, school compliance, program decisions, hiring and managing staff, and balancing the needs of other school administrators, teachers, students, parents, interest groups, and the community. However, unlike a corporate CEO, the superintendent has another very important role: cultivating a culture of shared vision and collaboration in which professional learning among educators can thrive.

According to researchers, these are some key strategies of a highly supportive superintendent:

- Schedule seminars and retreats to explore areas of difficulty and work as a superintendent-coach rather than a superintendent-director.
- Make professional learning a cycle of continuous improvement by integrating professional learning and reflection into day-to-day activities to find solutions to immediate problems.
- Recognize—and embrace—that all school stakeholders have different learning styles, abilities, preferences, and fears
- Offer mentor and coaching programs for new principals to build their capacity for instructional leadership.
- Encourage participants to build professional development portfolios to be shared with future candidates.
- Find ways, other than monetary rewards, to compensate staff for their professional learning efforts.

This list raises a question I believe deserves continual consideration: In what ways can the superintendent help develop a district culture supporting ongoing learning and creative thinking among staff?

Ongoing learning should be foundational in school districts, where the superintendent is responsible to empower teachers with the freedom to innovate. Although following and meeting all standards and state regulations is often difficult, superintendents can exercise creativity to develop a culture of disruptive innovation, fostering changes useful to teachers and students. Of course, there is no perfect formula to solve complex school problems, and a solution for one school may not necessarily work in another. Building-level professional learning can work well when the school's culture, population, and specific instructional needs are considered. Additionally, superintendents can refer to professional networks such as the American Association of School Administrators, Discovery Education, or The School Superintendents

Association's Digital Consortium for more suggestions about professional learning,

No educator needs to operate in isolation. This is why many groups of education professionals with the same interest and drive to change schools and education create PLNs. Here administrators and teachers can explore new ideas for their schools in a safe atmosphere with their peers, free from judgment or fear of consequences.

Kristine Gilmore, superintendent of Everest School District in Wisconsin, is an excellent example of a superintendent leading her district to change classroom instruction through intensive professional learning. The district's goal was to develop ways to use iPads to enhance learning among kindergarten through twelfth-grade students. Under Ms. Gilmore's leadership, teachers participated in professional learning experiences with the iPads so they could, in turn, help students use the devices in meaningful and creative ways. These experiences included "teachers teaching teachers best practices in the classroom, mini-courses on specific subjects, and three-day institutes focused on teaching and learning." The training was a success. By the end of the school year, the more than four hundred teachers in the district had accumulated more than 25,000 hours of professional learning, enabling them to comfortably meet the goal of using technology to enhance students' learning.

The superintendent plays a key role in helping district schools explore and accomplish their professional learning needs, as well as working with schools to create and implement a district-wide initiative. School districts can thrive because of the decisions their leaders make—decisions based on observation and evaluation of instruction and student achievement. The superintendent can set a supportive and positive tone and inspire district members to be ongoing learners who collaborate to solve challenges and make schools places where trust and kindness flourish in an environment meeting the diverse needs of each child.

SOCIAL MEDIA FOR PROFESSIONAL LEARNING

Principals also can cultivate teachers' desire to learn continually, encouraging them to use social media to develop a PLN, participating in Twitter, Facebook, Instagram, or other social media platforms.

Social media takes teachers and administrators beyond their schools' walls and current ways of thinking and processing information, opening doors to learning from other teachers, administrators, and nationally and internationally known educators. Before embarking on a social media journey, however, reflect on your why: why are you joining a social network, and what are your goals? Also important is following your school district's social media policy. For example, before posting photographs from your classroom on social media sites, be sure your school's policy doesn't prohibit this.

Social media platforms allow staff and administrators to learn valuable information, share with each other, and keep current on research-based studies. In addition, social media is a logical modern extension to communication with parents and the community to build their understanding and gain their support. I (Evan) support social media as a learning platform for schools and encourage my staff to use it as a way to keep parents, and the broader community, abreast of school initiatives and to celebrate the exciting happenings and innovative learning taking place. Our school has a Facebook page and a school website, where staff, students, and administrators can post things like this:

- Podcasts by students and staff
- Short videos about learning
- Interviews between a student newscaster and a teacher
- Student-led news
- Videos from the principal

PROFESSIONAL LEARNING IS THE CATALYST OF GROWTH AND CHANGE IN SCHOOLS THAT IMPACTS ADMINISTRATORS, STAFF, AND STUDENTS.

Everyone at school, along with parents and community supporters, can turn to these pages to learn about students, teachers, and special events.

My administrative and technology teams are also active on Twitter, always celebrating school happenings by sharing captioned photographs. We encourage staff to use Twitter, not only to learn and interact with other educators, but also as another vehicle to share with parents and other community members the unique and creative learning that our students experience.

Our goal is for staff to take charge of their professional learning through social media and other growth opportunities on the internet–free venues allowing them to learn from the best in education. I recommend TEDx Talks, videos, books, articles, and blogs to my staff and encourage them to share with colleagues. Whether learning as a group, in a team or department meeting, with a colleague during a common planning period, or while at home, these platforms can inspire and educate.

The more active staff members are on social media, the more they will benefit from the learning possibilities existing there. Educators can choose what they do on social media, resulting in a similar experience to that provided to students in progressive classrooms: choice and personalization. Inspiring information can lead to conversations stirring dreams of possibilities and energizing educators to build collective efficacy and growth mindsets among all players in a school district. Professional learning is the catalyst of growth and change in schools that impacts administrators, staff, and students.

REFLECT! DISCUSS WITH REVISIT! COLLEAGUES!

- How does the principal's leadership develop a school culture encouraging teachers to participate in professional learning networks?
- How do flipped faculty meetings foster professional learning and reflection on and changes in instruction?

—— **Share your thoughts and ideas! #teammakers** ——

CHAPTER 13
FOSTERING DISTRICT-WIDE PERSONAL AND COLLECTIVE EFFICACY

———

Lila, a first-year fifth-grade teacher, was having a tough time—and it was only October. Her principal asked me (Laura) to help. Because I had known Lila since she was in elementary school with my daughter, I recognized that she was a high achiever. I also knew that her dream was to become a teacher. The principal felt that since we already had a relationship, Lila would hear my suggestions.

Lila had recently graduated from college at the top of her class. The principal told me Lila had demonstrated had a high sense of efficacy during teacher training meetings, and he believed her strong work ethic and upbeat outlook would enable her to reach every child and help them progress. However, just six weeks into the school year, Lila was arriving at school at 7:00 a.m. and not leaving until 8:00 p.m., and dark rings under her eyes revealed erratic sleep patterns. When the principal told her that she had to leave by 6:00 p.m. and she needed a break from school, Lila disagreed. This is when I started meeting with her.

My goal was to help her develop personal efficacy, a belief that she had the capacity to reach the two goals we negotiated: (1) She could work on balancing her teaching and personal life and bring the wellness and positivity of this balance to students; and (2) She could develop the problem-solving skill needed to support her students. Hopefully, Lila could in turn bring efficacy and problem-solving to her students—skills they needed for success in school and life.

To give Lila an excuse to leave school early, I invited her to dinner and asked her to be at my home at 5:30 p.m. A few minutes after she walked into the kitchen, Lila burst into tears. "I can't do this. I'm a failure," she cried. "So many of my kids can barely read. I don't know what to do."

What had caused this dramatic change in Lila? She arrived at her first teaching position with high self-efficacy and, just over six weeks later, she no longer believed she was up to the challenge. Her words *I don't know what to do* revealed her problem: enthusiasm and self-efficacy weren't enough to support students reading far below grade level. Staying long hours at school and agonizing over her students weren't helping either.

Lila agreed to work with me, and a productive coaching relationship began. My goal was to offer support but also to build her knowledge about how to help students at diverse reading levels. Not unlike the experiences of many novice teachers, Lila's class included a large group of students reading one to three years below grade level. As I coached her about supporting striving readers, and we planned lessons together, Lila learned to meet the diverse needs of her students. Lila's teaching situation had diminished her enthusiasm and self-efficacy because, as she said, "I didn't have the skill set to help my students." Continual professional reading and coaching conversations with her colleagues and me not only enabled Lila to meet her students' needs but also to rebuild her enthusiasm for teaching.

Lila's story demonstrates that teachers with high enthusiasm and high self-efficacy also need the skill and experience to meet the challenges students pose. As Evan frequently says, "Limited skill sets of educators often compromise their personal efficacy." Fortunately, the opposite is also true.

THE POWER OF COLLECTIVE EFFICACY

Although coaching is one solution to supporting a novice teacher to maintain self-efficacy, other options also can be effective. The greatest difference, however, is made when the principal, staff, and other administrators value and create a school culture in which efficacy intertwines with professional learning. This environment builds trusting relationships and focuses all educators on students' success. If self-efficacy can empower individual teachers to work diligently and consistently to learn new ideas and set goals to challenge their students to improve and grow, imagine the trajectory of students' success when schools have *collective* teacher efficacy.

Internationally famous author, researcher, and speaker John Hattie is professor of education and director of the Visible Learning Labs, University of Auckland, New Zealand. According to Hattie's visible learning research, collective teacher efficacy is a formidable force. Hattie ranked one hundred fifty influences related to students' learning outcomes and determined the average effect size was 0.40. However, the effect size of collective teacher efficacy—the number-two influence on his list—was 1.57. Clearly, when teachers believe they can positively affect students' learning and create environments valuing relationships, trust, and professional study, they not only nurture the skill set needed to help students succeed, but they also honor students' dreams and stories.

How can school districts create collective teacher efficacy to empower educators to believe they can reach and support every learner? We have taken a deep dive into school divisions having high collective efficacy and identified several characteristics of the central office staff, principals, and teachers.

The Central Office. Collective efficacy begins with the central office staff. Whether districts are large or small, the collective efficacy of the superintendent and his staff has a direct effect on the efficacy of the staff in each school. Through their leadership, central office staff can raise efficacy levels with school administrators and staff:

- Forging positive, trusting relationships with staff and community
- Collaborating with school administrators to adjust curriculum and instruction
- Offering opportunities to develop leadership among staff
- Regularly visiting schools to observe teaching in action
- Generating enthusiasm for a shared school vision
- Valuing and funding professional learning
- Providing district-wide collaborative opportunities
- Spending more time doing *with* staff than doing *to* staff

In addition, central office staff can connect to schools by posting podcasts about successes, video messages, and updates on the school's website. Because principals' expectations of teachers—and teachers' expectations of students—should align with central office expectations, such actions help communicate the district's vision and mission as they develop efficacy among staff, principals, and other school administrators. Just as students work harder for adults they think like them, teachers and school administrators do the same in relation to superintendents and their staff. As such, we encourage central office staff to reflect on where connections with school personnel are strong and where they can be improved.

The Principal. To develop collective efficacy among staff, principals must be effective communicators who actively listen and collaborate with staff to coordinate ongoing professional learning, build trusting relationships, and encourage them to take risks and innovate. I (Evan) recognize that I must get out of my office and into classrooms, halls, the cafeteria, gym, and library to foster and maintain collective efficacy among staff. I listen carefully to teachers and students, and I follow-up conversations with email or a discussion in my office. I work daily to show everyone that my words, beliefs, actions, and decisions align with the agreed-on, collective vision of our school. To enlarge and maintain collective efficacy and a positive environment, I focus daily on these:

- Building a caring and trusting community by quickly responding to the needs of staff, students, and families
- Treating teachers as professionals by learning with them, providing opportunities to build their skill sets, and encouraging them to try creative ideas in their classes
- Fostering teacher leadership and advocacy
- Showing how much I care by knowing teachers' and students' dreams, stories, and goals
- Helping staff view problems as challenges to be overcome by working together
- Building school spirit and the feeling of "This is a great place to work!"

Teachers. Great teachers show self-efficacy *and* collective efficacy by embracing ongoing professional learning as the path to improving teaching and students' learning. They are highly enthused about teaching, whether presenting a mini-lesson, scaffolding students' learning, supporting a colleague, writing report cards, interacting with students, or keeping parents informed. Teachers with a high sense of efficacy believe that all students can learn, and these teachers can enlarge collective efficacy in these ways:

- Sharing teaching ideas with colleagues
- Mentoring new faculty
- Participating in professional learning and developing a PLN
- Remaining open minded to suggestions for improving instruction and accepting failures as information for progress
- Communicating positive energy to colleagues and students every day
- Making positivity a personal choice
- Reflecting daily on teaching, students' learning, and interactions with staff and parents to be self-evaluative and make adjustments
- Cultivating grit, a passion for reaching key goals, and a growth mindset

Equipped with personal and collective efficacy and the necessary skill set to make effective learning decisions and offer scaffolds, teachers empower students through a positive, student-centered environment in which they work primarily with small groups and individuals and provide helpful feedback. In his interlude, high school senior Sam Fremin explains how his teachers' perspectives on learning have empowered him and enlarged his self-efficacy.

STUDENT-TEACHER CONNECTIONS
An Interlude by Sam Fremin

Students can easily become frustrated with a teacher. Sometimes they see certain needs not being met, and they get discouraged. I've made more than my fair share of baseless assumptions about my teachers. I've either perceived from them a lack of attention to detail or negative feelings directed toward me. When I joined the #bowtieboys, now called #BOWTIE to include girls, I was prepared to get off my chest all sorts of negative anecdotes from my school experience. However, my explosive approach was diffused while presenting in our very first NCTE (National Council of Teachers of English) session.

Going in, I assumed that our goal was to show teachers what they didn't understand about students by having face-to-face conversations circling our stories of strong and weak classrooms. Instead, roles were reversed, and our panel served as teachers who facilitated discussion on our topics of classroom environment and differentiated learning. Surprisingly, our takeaways were far more mutual than I expected. Candidly speaking with teachers about their struggles with students and the educational world in general helped me see that a communication disconnect is often responsible for negative classroom ecologies. I get frustrated with teachers when I feel they don't understand why a strategy isn't connecting with me. On the other hand, teachers can feel frustrated with me and other students because taking multiple approaches isn't always successful.

Since joining the #BOWTIE, I have regularly participated in the #G2Great professional development forum on Twitter, providing similar experiences to my first NCTE conference. Moderators pose questions about teachers' tactics, and educators from around the country weigh in. I marvel at their responses. The enormous amount of caring these teachers possess for their students is palpable. Realizing this empowers me and the other students in the forum to interact more effectively with our own teachers and to assure them that we do yearn passionately for growth and progress.

The classrooms where I've felt the most comfortable advocating for myself are those in which this care from teachers is on full display. Teachers who are transparent about why they implement certain policies are also the most open to beneficial feedback, creating a safe environment for me to speak up and provide it. Ultimately, students and teachers work on the same team. Understanding why our teammates perform the way they do is essential to ensuring that the team can thrive.

SEVEN ACTIONABLE WAYS A PRINCIPAL CAN INCREASE EFFICACY

Principals are responsible for creating a school environment to enhance and nurture efficacy among staff and students. How can principals be more successful in this mission? The following are the top seven areas I (Evan) focus on to increase and positively impact the efficacy of my school community:

1. **Communication.** As noted above, principals must be active listeners and communicate genuine interest in staff members to build the relationships necessary to encourage efficacy.
2. **Visibility.** To interact and communicate, principals must be visible. Increased visibility leads to opportunities to engage with people and share beliefs about education, a current school initiative, or an important personal experience.
3. **Climate.** A supportive school climate sets the tone for people to be productive and positive about work. Climate alone does not make a school effective, but all successful schools have a healthy, positive climate. Reflect on these questions as you evaluate how you could improve the climate of your school:

   - How collaborative are you as a leader?
   - Is your school welcoming to the public?
   - As a principal, are you easily accessible?

4. **Positive attitude.** Great educational leaders choose a positive attitude. They communicate positive messages to students and staff about their capabilities to help them reach their individual potential. Additionally, they expect staff members to do the same. If a staff member is negative about students, let them know in a professional way that this is not acceptable. If you say nothing, you give the impression that you agree.
5. **Safety.** Staff and students perform best when they don't fear punishment or reprisal. A trusting environment in which staff and students feel safe fosters innovation and creativity, and it invites people to do their best.
6. **Professional learning.** Excellent professional learning equips teachers to be more effective and impact students' learning. Involve staff in professional discussions related to the learning experiences they need. Staff will appreciate being involved instead of being told what to do.
7. **Goal setting.** Work with staff to create goals meaningful to them and based on knowledge of students' progress and efficacy. Involving staff in goal creation empowers them and increases their ownership of the goals. Resist telling people what to do; goals rarely work when they are delivered as marching orders.

Principals set the tone, model the culture, and communicate the story of their school. The leader alone will not make an effective school, however. Effective school leaders also hire and retain teachers who collectively believe they can make a difference in the learning and lives of students. The collective efficacy the principal builds among teachers then trickles down to students, reinforcing their belief that hard work and continued effort will result in progress.

PRINCIPALS SET THE TONE, MODEL THE CULTURE, AND COMMUNICATE THE STORY OF EFFICACY.

Lao Tzu, a Chinese philosopher regarded as the founder of Taoism, said: "It is wisdom to know others; it is enlightenment to know one's self." His words lead us to deep understanding of collective efficacy by recognizing that efficacy requires both a knowledge of others and a knowledge of self. Armed with this understanding, administrators can not only better handle the day-to-day stresses of the job but, even more important, develop TeamMakers, create a collaborative school culture, resolve challenges, and foster growth through ongoing professional learning. When collective efficacy thrives in a school district, it empowers staff to learn from failures, be innovative, and focus on helping students experience success.

REFLECT! **DISCUSS WITH COLLEAGUES!** **REVISIT!**

- How can principals build and maintain collective efficacy at their schools?
- How does collective efficacy affect teachers' instruction and students' learning? How does it encourage reflection?

—— **Share your thoughts and ideas! #teammakers** ——

PART V
Walking the Tightrope of Change

Change can be scary. The initial reaction of some educators is to resist it. Feelings of "it worked for me, so it will work for my students" can no longer be a viable argument. Our students live in a world of rapid changes in technology and the ability to communicate globally. The skill set they need to solve community, national, and world problems includes critical and analytical thinking, teamwork, and the ability to communicate.

Evan and I want to support you on your journey, and to do that we share stories that illustrate the courage residing in each of us—the courage needed to change. We offer suggestions for advertising your message, telling your story, and enlisting the support of staff and community. You'll also find suggestions for becoming TeamMakers, collaborators who can transform schools into learning centers with skilled teachers and administrators who value reflection and can impact and shape how students learn.

We ask you to take charge of your professional learning, disrupt what's not working, and provide students with the expertise needed for the world they will inherit. To this end, we invite you to cultivate an open mindset and help develop students' creativity and imagination as well as their agency.

Finally, we offer concrete suggestions for getting started and moving forward on a journey that can impact leading, teaching, and learning. Both of us hope to inspire you to keep your dreams, hopes, and stories in your hearts and minds, but we also urge you to share them. We hope to inspire you to collaborate, communicate, and become the TeamMakers who can and will affect the changes needed in schools. When students graduate, they will need to have the empathy and compassion to communicate globally and also do good work for their community and the world.

CHAPTER 14
BUILDING A SCHOOL'S BRAND

———

Gary Dahl invented the Pet Rock in a bar in Los Gatos, California, after listening to friends complain about the time it took to care for their dogs and cats. His Pet Rock quickly became a sales phenomenon during the 1975 Christmas season. In fact, creative marketing—a rock packaged inside an appealing box—combined with Dahl generating a must-have demand among millions of Americans resulted in his selling more than five million rocks in six months! Dahl had created a *brand* sensation.

Using Dahl's marketing plan for the Pet Rock as a model for promoting a school may seem like a stretch, but several parts of the plan are applicable. By studying the Pet Rock fad, schools can discover Dahl's message about communicating and marketing a product and apply it to their own brand or stories. Consider the following aspects of the Pet Rock success:

- The marketing buzz created an "in" group—those possessing a rock were popular and hip. Because many Americans wanted to be "popular and hip," more and more people purchased Pet Rocks.
- This message was spread by word of mouth.
- People wanted the "official" Pet Rock, even though they could find similar ones in their own yards.

If marketing an ordinary rock can capture the attention of so many people, imagine the impact marketing a school's stories can make on families and the community. Can a school or entire division benefit from positive word-of-mouth buzz about staff, facilities, programs, and special events? Yes, it can! Just as Dahl created excitement about and a need for the Pet Rock, a community's enthusiasm can produce many benefits for a school and division, including support of budgets, programs, and facilities, to name a few.

Branding and marketing to the community should be part of every school's action plan. Each school has unique stories to tell about staff, students, academics, sports, fine arts and technology programs, annual learning initiatives, and special events. When schools communicate their stories to parents and the community, they promote their brand by celebrating inspiration and excellence. Schools committed to branding efforts build parent and community confidence and pride. Moreover, well-branded schools provide benefits to the community, such as creating the desire for people to purchase houses or run businesses near the school they want their children to attend.

To simplify branding, start by aligning what you want people to think about your school with what people actually value. Choose stories to move a school closer to congruency with those values. If there's a disconnect, view it as an opportunity to take action and improve.

ONE SMALL ACTION REAPS BIG RESULTS

For many years at my (Evan) school, our physical education teachers had a problem with students refusing to wear the school's P.E. uniforms. At first, we tried a traditional solution: students who didn't dress out for P.E. lost points from their final grade. But this didn't work; nothing changed.

One day the P.E. staff had a collective light-bulb moment. Perhaps students weren't dressing out because they felt the uniforms were ugly! I recall this as an "aha" moment, because my staff was thinking about a problem in a unique way. Instead of using punishment, they considered a new option: students might wear uniforms they liked.

To move the potential change process forward, I met with several student representatives, who quickly confirmed that they and their classmates disliked the uniforms. The P.E. staff and I decided to involve students in the design of new uniforms, hoping their participation would change their attitudes. We launched a contest to design new uniforms, and all students voted on a few of the designs they had developed. Since this day, we have had very few issues with students refusing to dress out for P.E. In fact, every day, I observe some students wearing their P.E. shirt and shorts to school because they really like them.

To change students' attitude toward school P.E. uniforms, my staff and I learned that we had to involve students—something we had not tried before. We also learned that how we communicate ideas to others and how they receive and interpret these ideas can affect perceptions and actions. The same is true for schools and their communities. When schools are innovative and purposeful in communicating their brand, they can positively impact the involvement of an entire school district and spark effective change.

We encourage schools to be intentional as they develop their brand. Intentional communication is thoughtful and planned, ensuring that the messages sent and stories told accurately define the school. Reflect on the following questions as you discuss effective communication:

- How is your school communicating positive information to students, staff, parents, and the community?
- What do current communication methods say about your school?
- What could be branded or rebranded in your school to build excitement among students and staff?

INTENTIONAL COMMUNICATION IS THOUGHTFUL AND PLANNED, ENSURING THAT THE MESSAGES SENT AND STORIES TOLD ACCURATELY DEFINE THE SCHOOL.

BRAND AND REBRAND

To help administrators, staff, and students reflect on how to communicate their school's brand—its unique story—we have identified eight key areas to explore. Gather feedback from stakeholders who use each one of these, and select three to four resonating with your needs to develop a plan to better communicate your school's stories to others. Remember, every message a school sends tells people what the principal and staff value and whether the school is friendly and inclusive, encourages kindness, builds trusting relationships, and has a positive, collaborative culture.

- **First impressions.** What do people see when they first walk in the front door of your school? Do they see a sign asking visitors to please report (not "must report") to the main office? Do they see walls celebrating student work? What visitors see when they enter a school can create a positive, welcoming tone.
- **Front office staff.** How does the front office staff interact with visitors? This can generate positive or negative feelings. Main office staff should be active listeners who offer a warm welcome to visitors, leaving them feeling positive about the school.
- **Websites and calendars.** Is information on school and class websites up to date? Keeping information current sends the message the administration and staff believe that informing families and community members about events and activities is important. We recommend having one person or a team responsible for continually updating the calendar to keep it current.
- **Teacher web presence.** Do teachers have a class web page where they can post student podcasts, pictures of students collaborating on projects, and videos of individual and group presentations? Because parents appreciate these windows into students' learning, encourage all teachers to create a class web page to share with parents how and what students learn.
- **Positive connections.** Is your staff making positive connections with families? By forging connections with families, schools create positive buzz in the community and develop an enthusiasm to increase parent support and participation. Encourage teachers to make at least two positive telephone calls to parents during the year to impact parents' pride in their children's learning. In addition, make parents feel welcome by inviting them to attend special school events.
- **Parent communications.** Does your school communicate regularly with families? Does your school have a schedule so that all grade-level teams and departments can include their

activities in parent newsletters on the website? Consistent and coordinated communication with parents should be every school's goal. Besides showing unity among teams, this communicates that the school values keeping families apprised of school happenings.

- **Collaboration.** Are staff and students included in decisions affecting school life? Does your school have student advisory groups? Does your school have clothing and other items students and staff can purchase to promote the school? We believe that promoting and communicating school spirit can enhance community support. Invite administrators, staff, and students to work in teams to promote school spirit and enthusiasm.
- **Social media.** Is your school using social media to share its values and beliefs and build your school's brand? Strive for balanced communication, and celebrate all school events and programs through Facebook, Twitter, and Instagram. We recommend that schools have one person or a small team to manage social media. Additionally, schools should define content expectations and develop recommendations for a minimal number of communications each day.

Scalability across a school division is part of effective branding. If one school in a division does an outstanding job communicating its brand and others do not, friction can develop between them. We suggest that school divisions consider purposeful and coordinated efforts to enhance branding of all schools and the central office.

TeamMakers poses a lot of questions that we hope you'll continually ask as you dream and work to improve or create something new in your schools. These questions can lead to reflection and shine a spotlight on your school's branding and rebranding needs. Telling your school's unique story starts with inspiration from central office leadership and moves to school administrators, staff, and students. Our vision is for all parts of a school to work together, collectively dreaming and storytelling. This is the ideal way to build a division's brand and rally parents and community around their school!

REFLECT! DISCUSS WITH COLLEAGUES! REVISIT!

- How does intentional communication help brand schools? What can your school do to become more intentional in its communication to staff, students, parents, and community?

- Are all schools in your division communicating a consistent message to parents and the community? Explain how your branding plan is scalable. If it is not, brainstorm ways to make it scalable.

—— Share your thoughts and ideas! #teammakers ——

CHAPTER 15
EVER-EVOLVING EDUCATORS

In 1922, at the age of sixteen, my (Laura) father, Sydney Seidner, left Krakow, Poland, boarded a ship, and entered the United States through Ellis Island. When he arrived in New York City, he could read and write Polish, and he could design and construct work shoes, dress shoes, and children's shoes because his parents had apprenticed him to a shoe-maker in Krakow when he was nine years old. He had enough money to live frugally for two months and rented a room in a family's apartment. Sidney registered to study English in a local high school and, although exhausted from working long hours in a shoe factory, he doggedly attended free English classes every night. One year later, he was able to speak, read, and write English. Two years later, he had saved enough money to bring his parents and sister to America.

My father's dream was to own a factory and design his own line of shoes. His evolving nature nudged him to learn more about shoes, and on most Saturdays, he took me to museums and department stores, where he studied shoes from the past and present. Just as writers carry a notebook to jot ideas, my father had a notebook for sketching shoes he liked and designing original ones. When Evan was nine, he began to accompany his grandfather on these "learning Saturdays."

Sidney Seidner's ever-evolving skills and strong work ethic pro-pelled him to realize his dream. He became the owner and designer of Erica Shoes, a company in lower Manhattan making shoes for high-end department stores and small boutiques.

A few months before his sixty-fifth birthday, my father suffered a heart attack. Forced to reduce his workload, he worked part-time for a while, and then retired. I (Evan) then watched my grandfather evolve and change again. He had a need and a drive to work and be productive, so after he retired, he taught himself how to design and make women's clothes. His home basement became a mini-factory, with shelves stacked with fabrics and leather filling one wall. He designed and made clothes for my mother and grandmother and made purses, wallets, and belts for the family.

ALTHOUGH IT'S IMPOSSIBLE TO PREDICT THE WORLD OUR STUDENTS WILL INHERIT, WE KNOW THEY WILL BE THE PROBLEM SOLVERS OF THEIR FUTURES.

My grandfather was a learner and a dreamer, and his life illustrates how evolving, growing, and changing can transform dreams into reality and maintain true purpose in one's life. He was creative and persistent, and he adjusted well to new situations. He felt empowered to adapt, grow, and develop the expertise to reach new goals. Today we would say he had a growth mindset and self-efficacy—a belief that he could adjust and reach his dreams.

Many of the lessons Sidney taught us are also applicable to educators. One of the most significant is to be an ever-evolving learner.

During my (Laura) first year of teaching, I was surrounded by several teachers who used the same lessons year after year. In fact, the science teacher told me, by the end of his third year, he had developed the lessons, board notes, quizzes, and tests he was still using twenty-five years later. Much had changed in science, but his students continued to copy the same notes from the board, complete the same worksheets, and take the same quizzes and tests. An example of a *non*-evolving teacher, he wasn't preparing students for *today*—much less for their future.

Our world continually changes, and although it's impossible to predict the world our students will inherit, we know they will be the problem solvers of their futures. They will have to tap into their creativity to find innovative solutions. Evolving teachers stay in touch with their own creativity and design learning experiences inviting their students to be creative. As Pamela Moran explains in her interlude, everyone is creative. Teachers are responsible to help students find and use their creativity.

CONTAGIOUS CREATIVITY
An Interlude by Pamela Moran, EdD

Observe toddlers play. Regardless of whether three-year-olds play with cardboard boxes, kitchen pots and pans, Play-Doh, or colorful markers, they can imagine it into something they can stack, hide in, smash, decorate, bang, or roll. You can almost see ideas jump from one toddler to another as they transition from parallel to associative to collaborative play.

As three-year-olds turn into five-year olds, they exhibit joy in discovering the world around them. Few preconceived notions shape how they use materials and resources to design, make, engineer, and build as they create with their hands and their minds. Wooden blocks in the hands of kindergarteners can quickly transform into a leaning tower, a castle, zoo, or boat. As children work together, you can almost see their creativity sparking a contagion of ideas.

However, if we observe those same kindergarteners as they become fourth, eighth, or twelfth graders, their creativity often appears to have faded away, unless they land in a classroom or school community where creative processes are valued. In these spaces, teachers encourage children to sustain curiosity, ask questions, pursue personal interests, find solutions to challenges, and reflect on their own learning as they engage. Moreover, when these spaces let educators' creative juices flow in the same way, they build a rich, experiential learning culture.

In this culture, the teacher or student creators need opportunities to reflect on the processes of their creation. They need to explore how they arrived at successful solutions, why they may have failed, and what they learned from both successes and failures. Through the creative processes—and the resulting failures and successes—students' knowledge and competencies will continue to evolve. In fact, the same creative processes a toddler applies to designing spaceships or submarines with cardboard boxes have been used to put astronauts on the moon, invent pacemakers, and write the "New World" symphony.

Everyone possesses creativity, even if it becomes buried over time. Schools have the power to unleash creativity or suppress it. When you encourage adults and children to offer their ideas to improve their world, they will generate new ways to think about solutions. They will see what others cannot and take risks to try new approaches. In fact, the culture of their school community will become one of contagious creativity: they will become designers, makers, builders, engineers, and inventors. Perhaps through this contagiously creative culture, students will learn to passionately dream about solutions to the grand challenges of the world, resulting in pursuing big ideas that make the world better for everyone.

BECOME AN EVOLVING EDUCATOR

Unfortunately, many American school teachers resemble those from the early 1900s. Many still set up their classroom seating in rows, stand at the board, and insist on students compliantly learning. However, when educators let go of practices that are no longer working, change can occur. When educators disrupt thought patterns they've accepted and use, change can occur. Educators' vision and reaction to change, combined with their desire to take charge of their learning, define how they teach and how students learn. Ultimately, schools change to better serve students.

TEACHING ISN'T STATIC. IT'S VITAL, VIGOROUS, AND CONTINUALLY EVOLVING.

Teaching isn't static. It's vital, vigorous, and continually evolving as more and more information about best practices becomes available. We view teaching as a journey with arrival points continually pushing us forward. As soon as educators feel they've reached the destination, learning, evolving, and growing stop.

To illustrate what an evolving educator looks like, we've listed ten characteristics to safeguard you from being enticed by sameness: same lessons, same materials, same notes, same tests, etc. We urge administrators and teachers to reflect on this list, a combination of what we learned from Sidney Seidner and our experiences. Then discuss and revisit it. These traits will enable you to tap into your creativity and adjust your craft based on your learning.

- **Be a lifelong learner.** Read professional articles and books. Develop a PLN. Share ideas with colleagues. Embrace teacher advocacy and agency.
- **Value creativity and imagination.** Dare to be different and enjoy out-of-the-box thinking. Take risks—imagine how your learning can affect your teaching. Nurture imaginative thinking and paint pictures of how you want to evolve and the learning experiences you'll offer students to develop their analytical and critical thinking.
- **Be collaborative.** The power of many minds in solving problems is greater than one mind. Collaboration can unleash creativity and help schools solve problems and plan for students' futures.
- **Cultivate an open mindset.** An open mindset supports exploring new ways of teaching and thinking about learning. Because openness removes or diminishes limitations, it can lead to change and personal growth.
- **Nurture personal efficacy.** Believe in your capacity to learn and evolve and reach goals through hard work, persistence, and collaboration.
- **Develop agency.** Think independently. Be in charge of your professional growth and contribute to the growth of your colleagues.
- **Create a positive school culture.** People who value relationships, kindness, trust, taking risks, and ongoing learning create a culture reflecting the same principles. In such a culture, everyone can evolve and actualize their dreams.
- **Be inspirational.** Develop positive relationships and inspire others to create, wonder, imagine, and grow.
- **Be persistent.** Don't give up. View failures as information to help you move forward.
- **Be professional.** Whether you are an administrator or teacher, view your position as an important career. Model professionalism and bring passion and commitment to what you do every day.

Helena, my (Laura) sixth-grade granddaughter, explained her school experience to me: "School is like eating. You bite and chew the words and ideas, and then you throw them up on the test. Two months later, you forget what you memorized." Even though the pace of change in educational research—what works best for learners—is fast, many educators aren't keeping abreast of the need for student-centered learning and asking students to think and analyze on a test.

Those who evolve with the changes will be the educational leaders who impact learning, efficacy, and school culture. We believe that stagnation and sameness hurts students and devalues the role of the professional educator. Students deserve passionate, committed teachers and administrators. Be the change. Dream and evolve into the administrator and teacher who prepares students for their future by helping them become lifelong thinkers and learners!

REFLECT! DISCUSS WITH COLLEAGUES! REVISIT!

- Review the list of ten characteristics of evolving educators. Reflect on your strengths and identify areas you need to develop.
- Is there consistency between your words and actions? If not, how might you improve?

—— **Share your thoughts and ideas! #teammakers** ——

CHAPTER 16
A REFLECTIVE, QUESTIONING MINDSET

This moment from my (Laura) first year of teaching fifth grade is forever imprinted on my mind. While monitoring lunch recess, I overheard several fifth graders whispering, "Caroline has cooties. Don't go near her." I wondered what I could do about this. Could I help the students understand that their statements were cruel? The situation worsened as we returned to our classroom. Most students steered as far as possible from Caroline, and her eyes brimmed with tears. In the moment I was both angry at the lack of compassion and kindness among students and upset that I had no satisfying solution. But I did have the chance to use my favorite strategy: delay in order to reflect. Once students were in their seats, I told them I was concerned about their behavior at recess. "We'll discuss this tomorrow morning," I told them, and I began the math lesson.

This strategy gave me time to reflect. I wondered whether Caroline would want to be present at the class meeting I planned to facilitate. I wondered how the other students would receive a replay of their comments. I wondered whether change would come soon or take time. The strategy also gave me time to analyze the situation and explore ways to improve it. Forcing the students to comply would only have resulted in their comments going underground, beyond the reach of teachers' ears. My goal was for students to make the decision to halt their hurtful behavior based on understandings developed through our discussions and their personal reflection.

Caroline opted out of all the meetings and spent the time reading in the library. She chose this option because she felt she didn't need to be hurt by their comments again. Since third grade, Caroline had become the outsider in this class. She couldn't tell me an event or situation that caused this, but her classmates, together since kindergarten, did not accept her. Change in students' attitudes finally arrived after several class meetings.

Reflection and raising questions are important to education. They support teachers, administrators, and district-wide initiatives. More effective actions and decisions often result from reflection and wondering than those made in the moment. Delaying quick decisions has worked well in our experience because it buys time to review the experience or situation and gain the perspective needed to understand it and generate ideas for dealing with it. Moreover, delay also provides students time to mull over what happened and connect to and assess the feelings they had during and after the event.

Reflection is a powerful learning and imagining tool. It enhances experiences by reclaiming related memories, deepening insights, helping people make sense of new information, and making it possible to use prior knowledge to create new understandings. Those who reflect experience joy in reading, learning, and daily life. They also develop agency and the capacity for positive change.

Reflection and raising questions are tools all stakeholders in a school division can use to support administrators, school staff, and students coping with daily challenges. This kind of reflection and questioning is situational and supports the following:

- Teachers' practice and their understanding of students
- The principal's interactions with staff, students, and parents
- The principal's engagement with school-wide initiatives, instruction, communication, and technology
- The superintendent's vision for the district, needs observed in schools, and district-wide initiatives

THE REFLECTIVE PRINCIPAL

The reflective principal solves problems relating to staff, parents, and student issues by raising questions and setting aside time to think—perhaps at school or at home, or while driving to and from school. Often, I'll (Evan) take several minutes alone in my office to reflect on a recent issue or to mull over a challenge staff is pressing me to address. These quiet moments enable me to think creatively about these situations.

As a new principal, I faced the challenge of teachers feeling I would criticize them, as past administrators had, for allowing students to read self-selected books. My goal was for teachers to understand that I greatly valued independent reading and hoped they would include it in their ELA classes. I reflected on what I could do to change their mindset. First, I met with ELA teachers and explained that I highly valued independent reading of self-selected books during class. At subsequent meetings, I shared research about independent reading developing lifelong readers and literary tastes, but also how it enlarged students' vocabulary and background knowledge. In addition, I released funds to enlarge class libraries so students could choose from a wide range of genres and books relevant to their lives. I discovered that, as a result of my openly sharing the importance of independent reading and encouraging teachers to make it part of their reading curriculum, the teachers quickly changed their outlook.

Some challenges, however, aren't this easy to solve, and some aren't solved during a single school year. For example, when a school faces a situation such as bullying, parents and community members frequently blame the school and become extremely vocal. Through reflection, schools can identify ways to minimize bullying and emphasize positive, compassionate behaviors. When I faced this concern, I identified a few research-based programs to address bullying, and the guidance department organized a committee, including me, to review each program and recommend one to the staff. In addition, staff decided to devote the fifth day of our micro block to class meetings, allowing students to openly and confidentially discuss issues they faced at school.

THE REFLECTIVE TEACHER

The reflective teacher develops the habit of thinking about lessons and students' learning during planning periods, recess, lunch, and at the end of each school day. In fact, even if teachers have to wait for a lull in their schedule to formally reflect, often an idea for handling a situation will suddenly pop into their minds because their brains have been working hard to resolve the issue until time to raise questions and reflect was available.

Although I (Laura) continue to reflect on my lessons and how each one affects students' learning, my use of reflection started early in my career. The first time I learned with students in fifth grade reading at an early first-grade level, I could barely tread water. My reflections pointed me to one challenge: even though these students had experienced synthetic phonics programs, they couldn't hear short and long vowels, nor could they pronounce consonant digraphs (th, sh, ch, wh) and many blends (dr, spl, gl, sm, st, etc.). They had never read an entire book on their own; they had only experienced books through teachers reading them aloud.

My reflections sent me back to a class I had taken on word study, using *Words Their Way* (Pearson, 2011) as the primary text. I spent much of a weekend rereading my class notes, sections of the book, and doing several word sorts recommended in the book. This reflection returned me to information and experiences I had not used for several years and ultimately shaped the way my present students and I learned together. As I introduced my students to this kinesthetic experience of sorting words by pattern and understanding the meaning of each word in a sort, I hoped it would develop their decoding abilities. And it did! In addition, during short mini-lessons, we played with the diverse forms of words students sorted each week. For example, while studying long "o" patterns, students and I played with the word *float* and built this set of words: *float, floated, floating, floatation,* and *refloat.*

Asking myself, "How can I enlarge students' word knowledge?" led me to introduce multiple forms of words each time we worked on a new sort. Reflection and observation taught me that students frequently needed to spend two weeks with a sort instead of the recommended one week. Reflecting on specific teaching and learning situations can result in developing strategies and interventions that meet the needs of a specific group of students.

The teachers I coach and learn with at Daniel Morgan Intermediate School in Winchester, Virginia, often share their reflections with me, especially when they want additional feedback. Wanda Waters shared questions she had raised about José, a student in her Pathways class: *Why wasn't he completing work? Why did he put his head on the desk and sometimes fall asleep? Why didn't the daily read-aloud interest him?*

Wanda explained that when she asked José why he seemed so tired, he put his head down, looked at the floor, and said nothing. Together, we developed an intervention plan, including my getting to know José and administering to him an Independent Reading Inventory (IRI). After three meetings with José, I learned that he had books and read at home, but he had difficulty falling asleep and often awoke early. After conducting the IRI with José, I found that his instructional level was mid third grade. He also shared he only liked reading books he chose.

REFLECTING ON SPECIFIC TEACHING AND LEARNING SITUATIONS CAN RESULT IN DEVELOPING STRATEGIES AND INTERVENTIONS THAT MEET THE NEEDS OF A SPECIFIC GROUP OF STUDENTS.

Our first accommodations included moving José to the front of the classroom to help him better connect with daily read-alouds. In addition to giving José choice in his independent reading, Wanda tried as much as possible to offer his guided reading group choices as well. She frequently asked José about his sleep patterns and, when a lack of sleep persisted, she contacted the school nurse and guidance counselor, who contacted José's parents.

As Wanda demonstrated, if your questions and reflections aren't adequately supporting a student, don't give up. Ask a colleague or a coach, if your school has one, to weigh in and put fresh eyes on the situation.

REFLECTIVE CENTRAL OFFICE STAFF

When central office staff reflect and raise questions based on school visits and principals' feedback, they can better collaborate with school staff and administrators to support positive change. As I (Laura) mentioned in an earlier chapter, Dr. Van Heukelum, Superintendent of Winchester Public Schools, funded class libraries for ELA teachers in grades five and six at Daniel Morgan Intermediate School (DMIS) after school visits and discussions with the principal of DMIS helped him recognize this need. When I suggested to Dr. Wygal, principal of DMIS, and Dr. Van Heukelum that it also would be beneficial to have libraries in math, science, and social studies classes to send the message to students that reading was important in all subjects, both were on board. Dr. Van Heukelum funded class libraries for these subjects in the fifth and sixth grades, with teachers each ordering two hundred fifty books!

When the books arrived at the school, Dr. Van Heukelum joined the teachers to unpack the boxes that had been checked into the school. Teachers were excited because Dr. Van Heukelum supported them and enthusiastically participated in the project. In fact, his support extended to asking me to lead a workshop about how to use the books with students. Reflection led this superintendent not only to support this effort through funding, but it moved him beyond funding to collaborating and learning with teachers, demonstrating by his actions how important access to books and reading was for students in all subjects. His support, enthusiasm, and level of participation—all resulting from reflection—will likely have a lasting impact on how teachers integrate these books into their curriculum.

Reflective central office administrators also spend time each day in schools and develop relationships with teachers and students, enabling them to pose questions leading to reflection and change. Dr. Marc Ferris, Assistant Superintendent of Instruction for Wantagh Public Schools, spends much of his time visiting classes and listening to teachers. During his visits to middle school ELA teachers, Dr Ferris observed that teachers felt frustrated trying to teach reading and writing in daily forty-minute periods. To support teachers, Dr. Ferris studied the school schedule, reflected on a few options, and found a way to set up sixty-minute ELA periods on Mondays, Wednesdays, and Fridays, and forty-minute classes on Tuesdays and Thursdays. He brought his plan to the principal, who wanted to start with the change for grade six and add the change for grades seven and eight the following school year. In addition to the schedule changes, Dr. Ferris and the superintendent set aside funds for class libraries and genre units of study, and they hired me to work with teachers.

When central office administrators are in schools listening to the principals, teachers, and students, they become aware of specific challenges and needs and can use reflection and questioning to generate possibilities for positive change. They can also bring more positivity to a school's culture and collaborate to improve instruction and students' learning.

THE REFLECTIVE STUDENT

Opportunities for teachers to encourage students to reflect often occur during guided reading or while teachers meet with pairs of students or individuals. Recently after fifth grader Gracie and her group finished reading *Stone Fox* by John Reynolds Gardiner, she closed her eyes for a few moments, expressing the hope that more pages would pop into the book. "There has to be more!" she blurted out. "It can't end. I want to know what happened after Searchlight died." Gently, Mrs. Yost, Gracie's teacher, reminded her she could extend the end of the story in her mind, imagining what else could happen. She could continue to think about and reflect on what she had learned from the characters and events.

Gracie and her teacher illustrate reflecting about reading in the moment and how reflection can boost students' connections to characters, conflicts, problems, and new information. But it can do more. In Gracie's situation, she developed empathy for orphans and children shouldering adult responsibilities.

Teachers also can offer students opportunities to reflect on and self-evaluate their work. Every four to six weeks, students can select a piece of writing from their folders or readers' notebooks demonstrating their progress and write about the improvement they observe. It's helpful to invite students to brainstorm the mini-lessons presented and what they practiced and applied to their reading and writing. This exercise provides students with ideas to choose from when completing their self-evaluations. Teachers who offer students time to pause, reflect on their work, and write about their observations help them develop analytical skills for thinking about learning and progress—something they don't automatically do.

COLLECTIVE REFLECTION

In addition to individual reflection and questioning, we also have experienced the value of collective reflection—pairs and groups generating questions and mulling over each one to create change or resolve a common challenge. I (Evan) continually strive to address school challenges by inviting staff to join me in raising questions and reflecting. Several years ago, my school lost transportation funding for an after-school academic support program. At first, we tried to maintain the program by asking families to pick up their children; however, this didn't work because most parents had jobs, and some didn't have a car. I posed this question to staff: *How can we bring this program back but schedule it during the school day?* At our first meeting, we generated questions:

- Do we still have a large group of students who need extra academic support?
- How can we fit this into the schedule? What schedule changes can be made?
- How will other teachers view these changes? Will there be high or minimal resistance?
- Can this time also be used for students who would benefit from enrichment?

My staff had always been committed to enrichment but had not considered a separate enrichment class, so I created a committee to reflect and problem solve. The committee looked at all the challenges and decided to recommend taking a few minutes off each class block and adding a thirty-five-minute micro block for all students. The teachers and I created four flexible tiers for this new block, ranging from intensive remediation in math and reading to academic enrichment, and we agreed that students would move in and out of a specific tier based on their progress and teacher recommendations.

Reflection is a discipline you must practice, nurture, and cultivate. Eventually it becomes part of how you distill learning, interactions, reading, writing, and life experiences. Generating questions, combined with reflection, often leads to innovation—finding unique and useful solutions to challenges and supporting interventions. This process taps into the creativity everyone has. All stakeholders in a school district can use wondering and reflection to think, learn, and connect. We encourage you to become a reflective practitioner who questions and collaborates to develop student-focused, compassionate, and empathetic school communities valuing creative thinking and innovation.

REFLECT! **DISCUSS WITH COLLEAGUES!** **REVISIT!**

- How does reflection improve your teaching and understanding of students' needs?
- How has reflection supported deeper connections with members of your school and district?
- Discuss how wondering and reflection have connected you to creativity and innovation.

—— **Share your thoughts and ideas! #teammakers** ——

CHAPTER 17
GETTING STARTED AND MOVING FORWARD

We began this book by shining a spotlight on dreaming, wondering, and sharing stories as positive ways for all members of a school district to connect and forge relationships. The goal is to dream big—but start small. This can help districts adjust and refine their collaborative process and reach their goals. Our dream is for all schools in a district to work together to make significant change in their culture and instructional practices. This can occur when administrators cultivate a shared vision among staff, identify a need for change, and collaborate to develop a plan, looking carefully and deeply at how to achieve a shared goal.

To nurture and maintain a team spirit valuing input from all school district members, we suggest that you start with an initiative affecting everyone. Moreover, because the culture and climate of schools within a district differ, it's important to develop a process offering each school a voice. Successfully implementing a district-wide initiative can take two or more years, and time frames for individual schools might differ. In addition, large districts might focus on one group of schools at a time: elementary, middle, or high schools. In the following sections of this chapter, we will outline the process for moving forward with making changes within a district.

THE PROCESS OF CHANGE

Identifying initiatives. The first step in this process is to identify an initiative for your district to pursue and then set up the two meetings suggested below:

- The superintendent and designated office staff meet with the principals of each school to discuss organizing teams of teachers representing all subjects and grades.
- Central office personnel then meet with each principal and staff at their schools to discuss possible district-wide initiatives and select the top two.

We recommend keeping notes of ideas presented during the discussion. Principals then share their schools' top two initiatives with the central office and collaborate to select the four or five most popular initiatives of all those submitted. Teachers and administrators are then invited to vote on those top four or five to determine the initiative they want to pursue.

As we continue to explore the collaboration and communication that school districts can use to implement a specific initiative, we will use the initiative of *creating a district-wide culture of reading* as an example to illustrate the components of the change process.

Launching the initiative.

- Using the initiative of building a culture of reading in every school, the superintendent invites schools' administration and staff to consider their specific needs.
- Each school shares its list of needs via email.
- Ask a teacher and administrator to volunteer to extract, from the lists of needs sent from all schools, those that are common to all schools. Create a second list of items specific to schools. Email this list to everyone.

To involve students in creating a culture of reading in their schools, teachers and administrators can select a few student representatives or invite those in student government positions to participate. Students can meet with the principal and a group of teachers to discuss issues surrounding the initiative relevant to their learning. For example, students can suggest titles of books they'd like to see in class and school libraries. Or they might have ideas about scheduling to allow for independent reading of self-selected books along with instructional reading.

Several areas must be investigated for a district-wide initiative to be implemented, including materials, scheduling, professional learning, coaching, and funding. In addition to discussing each of these in light of our example initiative of creating a culture of reading, we've also generated questions related to each area to reflect on and discuss. However, we recognize that our list of questions may not address your situation. Feel free to add questions and adjust those we've suggested.

Schools will separately identify their needs for each item and then choose representatives from administration and staff to meet with central office staff to share and discuss their findings. The goal is to collaborate, communicate, and develop a plan. This phase will require more than one meeting.

Identify materials needed. Class libraries should have books in a variety of genres representing the cultural diversity in the school and a broad range of students' interests. We recommend that class libraries have a minimum of six hundred books and suggest that teachers increase this to one thousand over a time frame reasonable for the district. Having both a school library and class libraries is a benefit. Libraries in classrooms provide students with books at their fingertips so when they complete one, they can return it and choose a new book. The school library has a much larger and diverse collection of books than students find in the classroom. Selecting books from both libraries gives students more reading choices and enables them to develop relationships with both their teacher and the librarian, two people who can support their personal reading lives and nurture a love of reading. Consider the following questions for reflection and discussion:

- Does the central library need more diversity in reading levels and genres?
- Does the central library provide collaborative spaces for students?
- Do class libraries need to be purchased for ELA classes and content area classes?
- Do classrooms need shelving for books?
- What are the demographics and interests of students?
- How will this affect the books purchased for class libraries?

- What suggestions do students have for adding new books to the library?
- Why is it important for students to set up the class libraries?
- What is the best way to organize class libraries?
- How can teachers keep track of books checked out and returned?

Making schedule adjustments. To develop a culture of reading in all schools, students need to have time to read self-selected books at school. Giving students time to read at school tells students that teachers and administrators value independent reading. In addition, researchers have shown a correlation between time spent on independent reading and reading achievement. Equally important, students who read self-selected books every day, according to the research of Richard Allington and Stephen Krashen, are more likely to become lifelong readers. Consider the following questions for reflection and discussion:

Does the present schedule allow students to read self-selected books at least three times per week in class?
- How can we adjust schedules so independent reading happens at school?
- Should a team of teachers and administrators visit schools to study alternative schedules offering more daily ELA time?
- If the schedule does change, what kind of training will teachers need?
- What are some benefits of central office administrators reflecting on present schedules and suggesting alternatives for schools to consider?

Provide additional professional learning. As we've already stated in Chapter 12, we believe professional learning at the building level should be ongoing throughout the school year. However, when a district collaborates to adopt an initiative affecting everyone, professional learning, specifically focused on the initiative, can be an insurance policy for success. For our example initiative of creating a culture of reading in schools, we would encourage schools to purchase professional books for groups to study and to recommend important online articles and videos to read, watch, and discuss. It's also beneficial for teachers to read and discuss outstanding books for students in kindergarten through grade twelve.

Teams and departments can select the same book or choose different ones. Keep groups small so all members can share ideas.

Through book studies, teachers experience important elements of literary discussions: active listening, politely challenging an interpretation, finding text support, deepening their knowledge of a genre, and completing informal writing about reading. In turn, they can transfer these elements to their work with students. Hopefully, some might form groups that regularly read and discuss outstanding literature. Consider the following questions for reflection and discussion:

- Will it be necessary to hire a long-term consultant to work in schools and support the initiative?
- Are schools inviting teachers to suggest books and articles for small group studies?
- Do teachers have choice in the book they read and group they join?
- When will book discussions occur?
- Can some book discussions be posted online?
- Why is it important for administrators to join book discussions?
- Why is it beneficial for teams or departments to watch videos together?
- Why is it okay for individual schools to organize professional learning differently?
- Why should a few professional learning days for administrators and teachers be part of the yearly calendar?

Provide coaching support. When schedules change or when the goal is for students to become more involved and invested in their learning, coaches can provide support to diminish teachers' fears and anxiety. Because the coach often plans and teaches lessons with a teacher, it's possible to change and adjust instruction so a culture of reading flourishes. Consider the following questions for reflection and discussion:

- Why is it important for each school to have coaches who can support teachers?
- How can schools use experienced teachers as coaches without adding to their workload?
- How will instruction change if a schedule change creates longer class periods?

- How can a coach help teachers model how to select books for independent and instructional reading?
- Why is support from a coach beneficial for teachers in moving toward a student-centered approach?

Finding the funds. Generating and reflecting on questions can spark discussions about how much money each school in a district will need annually to continue building a culture of reading. Likely, the amount of annual funding required by each school will vary. The superintendent and budget manager can meet with principals to determine funding needed for the initiative and to what extent the district's budget can support the needs. In addition, principals can collaborate to explore ways to find additional money. Consider the following questions for reflection and discussion:

- Is it possible to increase funding for the initiative during the second and third years?
- Are there grants available to support the initiative?
- Are there teachers and administrators who would volunteer to collaborate and investigate potential grants and apply for them?
- How can parent organizations raise money for books?

Revisit, review, and refine. Whether implementing an initiative takes one, two, or three years, it's crucial for staff and administrators to continually review the process to adjust what's not working and add new ideas that surface during implementation. Like an individual going to a doctor for bi-annual checkups because physical needs change, schools' needs also change. New hires will require training, materials will need updating, or student enrollment might increase and create a need for enlarging class libraries. Revisiting initiatives allows schools to maintain established goals.

Districts will become expert jugglers, using observations, shared experiences, and students' feedback to revisit and refine the effectiveness of one initiative while embarking on a journey to address a new one. Like juggling, the more practice a district has, the easier it is to maintain the flow and progress of more than one initiative.

We believe that students' learning improves when districts collaborate on initiatives. We presented one example initiative so you can see how collaboration among all district members can bring about significant change. However, the plan we shared is not carved in stone. It is flexible, and we invite you to adapt it to your school's culture and needs.

"ONE BOOK, ONE COMMUNITY"

Another small step toward a district working together to make significant change is to initiate a district-wide book study. When an entire school district bands together to read and discuss one book during a school year, new relationships and friendships develop, and new ways of thinking occur. Books such as *Drive: The Surprising Truth about What Motivates Us* by Daniel Pink (Riverhead Books, 2011) motivate and affect the decisions leaders, teachers, and parents make every day. We recommend that you choose a school community book at the end of a school year, so you can order copies and organize the study over the summer. We've recommended at the end of this book several titles appropriate for teachers, administrators, and other school staff.

The superintendent can select the book, but we prefer a different strategy. We recommend that the superintendent meet with principals, select three books, and then invite all administrators and teachers to vote for their favorite two choices. Select the book receiving the most votes and order it. We also suggest that schools form partnerships with administrators and teachers from another school in their district. Principals of both schools can work with their team leaders and department chairs to create a reading and discussion schedule and share it with central office staff so they can also participate. In smaller districts, all staff can meet after completing the book to discuss what they learned, lingering questions, and how the book's content affects their leadership and teaching. Large school districts can ask schools to compile a list of what they've learned, lingering questions, and changes in leadership and teaching to share with other schools.

Because "one book, one community" is a huge undertaking for a district, consider doing it only every two to three years. Nevertheless, the benefits far outweigh the effort to coordinate the study. One district I (Laura) worked with studied *Drive* by Daniel Pink, and their discussions led them to question several of their practices:

- Students reading books for points and receiving rewards such as pizza and ice cream parties

- Some teachers using behavior charts to develop a culture of compliant students
- Schools following rigid pacing guides requiring teachers to complete a chapter or unit on a specific date

The book study opened minds to alternate ideas as groups discussed how they could replace and adjust present practices. Many began to move from a culture of compliance to one of engaging students in their learning. Additionally, the study helped them to slowly relinquish fixed mindsets and replace them with growth mindsets. The book study did even more:

- Forged new relationships among teachers
- Enabled participants to develop collective questions about accepted teaching and learning practices
- Highlighted the benefits of collaborative discussions to effect change
- Opened a dialogue leading to positive change
- Illustrated the benefits of professional learning
- Created a large support system for implementing changes
- Developed a desire for change

Additionally, during district-wide book studies and discussions, teachers and administrators self-reflect, dream, generate ideas, share stories and beliefs, and form relationships that can build collective efficacy and mindsets made for change.

TAKING THIS JOURNEY TOGETHER BECOMES A DISTRICT-WIDE ODYSSEY OF TEAMMAKERS WHO CAN TRANSFORM SCHOOLS INTO EVER-EVOLVING LEARNING CENTERS.

We call our book *TeamMakers* because we hope school districts will see themselves as one team dedicated to serving all students. The stories about Dr. Van Heukelum and the interludes by Dr. Kris Felicello, Dr. Mark Ferris, and Marlena Gross-Taylor illustrate how invested and team-minded central office administrators can positively impact school leaders, staff, and students. Taking this journey together becomes a district-wide odyssey of TeamMakers who can transform schools into ever-evolving learning centers. Together we can empower one another to learn, collaborate, communicate, analyze data, and think critically. Armed with this skill set, we can prepare students to be reflective and critical thinkers as well as lifelong learners who can become the creative problem solvers their future world will need.

REFLECT! DISCUSS WITH COLLEAGUES! REVISIT!

- Why is district-wide collaboration an effective way to achieve creative, positive change?
- Identify and discuss what your next steps will be.

—— **Share your thoughts and ideas! #teammakers** ——

QR CODE FOR PODCAST
TEAMMAKERS, MOVING FORWARD

RECOMMENDATIONS FOR DISTRICT-WIDE BOOK STUDIES

- *Culturize: Every student. Every Day. Whatever It Takes* by Jimmy Casas, Dave Burgess Consulting, Inc., 2017
- *Drive: The Surprising Truth about What Motivates Us* by Daniel Pink, Riverhead Books, 2011
- *The Innovator's Mindset: Empower Learning, Unleash Talent, and Lead a Culture of Creativity* by George Couros, Dave Burgess Consulting, Inc., 2015
- *Lead with Culture: What Really Matters in Our Schools* by Jay Billy, Dave Burgess Consulting, Inc., 2018
- *Learning Transformed: 8 Keys to Designing Tomorrow's Schools Today* by Eric Sheninger, ASCD, 2017
- *Outliers: The Story of Success* by Malcolm Gladwell, Back Bay Books, 2011
- *The 7 Habits of Highly Effective People: Powerful Lessons in Personal Change* by Stephen R. Covey, Free Press, 2014

BIBLIOGRAPHY

Allington, Richard L. "How Reading Volume Affects Both Reading Fluency and Reading Achievement." *International Electronic Journal of Elementary Education*. 7, no. 1 (2014): 13-26.

Bear, Donald R., Marcia R. Invernizzi, Shane R. Templeton, and Francine Johnston. *Words Their Way: Word Study for Phonics, Vocabulary, and Spelling Instruction*, 5th edition. New York, NY: Pearson, 2011.

Bennis, Warren. *On Becoming a Leader*, 4th edition. New York, NY: Basic Books, 2009.

Daniels, Smokey. *Literature Circles: Voice and Choice in Book Clubs and Reading Groups*, 2nd edition. Portsmouth, NH: Stenhouse, 2002.

Dewey, John. *Democracy and Education*. New York, NY: Macmillan, 1944.

Dweck, Carol S. *Mindset: The New Psychology of Success*. New York, NY: Random House, 2007.

Gardener, John R. *Stone Fox*. New York, NY: Harper Trophy Books, 2010.

Graham, Steve, Harris, Karen R. Santangelo, Tanya. "Research-based writing practices and the Common Core: Meta-analysis and Meta-synthesis." In *Elementary School Journal*, 115, 498-522, 2015.

Hattie, John. "The Applicability of Visible Learning to Higher Education." In *Scholarship of Teaching and Learning in Psychology* 1, no. 1 (2015): 79-91.

Kirr, Joy. *Shift This!: How to Implement Gradual Changes for Massive Impact in Your Classroom*. San Diego, CA: Dave Burgess Consulting, Inc., 2017.

Krashen, Stephen D. *The Power of Reading: Insights from Research*, 2nd edition. Westport, CT: Libraries Unlimited and Portsmouth, NH: Heinemann, 2004.

Merriam, Eve. "A Lazy Thought" In *There Is No Rhyme for Silver*, illustrator, Joseph Schindelman, New York, NY: Atheneum. 1962.

Sheninger, Eric. "QuotED." www.bamradionetwork.com/QuotED

Sinek, Simon and Kubassek, Jay. "An Amazing Conversation Between Simon Sinek and Jay Kubassek." https://jaykubassek.com/an-amazing-conversation-between-simon-sinek-and-jay-kubassek/

Robb, Laura. *READ TALK WRITE: 35 Lessons That Teach Students to Analyze Fiction and Nonfiction*. Thousand Oaks, CA: Corwin, 2017.

Wells, Gordon. *The Meaning Makers: Children Learning language and Using Language to Learn*. Portsmouth, NH: Heinemann, 1985.

ACKNOWLEDGMENTS

It takes a village to develop an idea for a book and then write the book. Evan and I thank all the educators and students who have touched our lives and shaped our thinking. A special thanks to Cookie Robb who supported us with encouragement and by helping us find the time we needed to generate ideas and write together.

Deepest thanks to the educators who wrote an Interlude: Dr. Kris Felicello, Dr. Marc Ferris, Marlena Gross-Taylor, Dr. Pamela Moran, Dr. Milton Ramirez, Wand Waters, Bridget Wilson, and Stacey Yost. A special shout out of thanks goes to Jason Augostowksi, high school English teacher in northern Virginia and organizer of the #BOWTIE. With Jason's guidance and suggestions, three high school students, Sam Fremin, Joe O'Such, and Leila Mohajer have each written an Interlude show-casing their excellent knowledge of teaching and learning.

Finally, we thank Shelley and Dave Burgess for their encouragement, and for their understanding that all stakeholders in a school division need to dream, share stories, learn, and work as a team to make positive changes. We truly appreciate that both Shelley and Dave recognize the importance of preparing students for their future by developing their ability to collaborate, communicate, think critically, and tap into their creativity in order to solve problems they will face as they continue their education and/or start their careers.

CONTRIBUTING AUTHORS

Marlena Gross-Taylor is Chief Academic Officer for Douglas County School District in Castle Rock, Colorado. She is also a consultant, founder of EduGladiators, and a blogger.

Lelia Mohajer is a ninth grader at Riverside High School in Leesburg, Virginia, who plays volleyball and enjoys fine arts, acting in school productions, and being a #BOWTIE!

Dr. Marc Ferris is assistant superintendent of instruction for Wantagh Public Schools in Wantagh, New York.

Wanda Waters, **Bridget Wilson**, and **Stacey Yost** are members of the fifth-grade team at Daniel Morgan Intermediate School in Winchester, Virginia. As teacher leaders, they advocate for students and love learning about the art and craft of teaching.

Dr. Kris Felicello is assistant superintendent for educational services in North Rockland Central School District in Garnerville, New York.

Joe O'Such is a junior at Riverside High School in Leesburg, Virginia, and has been a member of the #BOWTIE since 2015. With the #bowtieboys, he's hosted nationwide Twitter chats and attended and participated in several NCTE conventions. He also runs cross country and track and tutors elementary school children at his church.

Dr. Milton L. Ramirez is a longtime educator and a former math teacher in Ecuador and St. Mary of the Assumption High School in Elizabeth, New Jersey. Presently he is the Curriculum Design and Instructional Decision Making Instructor at University of the People.

Sam Fremin is a high school senior at Stonebridge High School in Ashburn, Virginia. As a member of the #BOWTIE for the last five years, Sam has used his voice to be an advocate for increased student representation in all aspects of the classroom. In addition to working with the #BOWTIE, he is a constant presence in his school's drama department and an avid tweeter.

Dr. Pamela Moran served as superintendent of Albemarle County Schools in Virginia for more than a decade. Presently, she is the executive director of the Virginia School Consortium for Learning.

ABOUT THE AUTHORS

LAURA ROBB

Author, teacher, coach, and international speaker, Laura Robb has completed more than 43 years of teaching in grades 4–8, and she returns to teach striving readers each year. Robb received the Richard W. Halle Award for outstanding middle level educator from NCTE as well as the Friends of Literacy Award from the Nassau Reading Council.

Laura Robb has written more than 30 books for teachers. Recent books are: *The Reading Intervention Toolkit*, by Shell Education and *Read Talk Write: 35 Lessons That Teach Students to Analyze Fiction and Nonfiction*, published by Corwin Literacy. Corwin Literacy also published *Robb's Vocabulary Is Comprehension: Getting to the Root of Complex Texts*.

Her newest for Heinemann is a First Hand Curriculum: *Smart Writing: Practical Units For Teaching Middle School Writers*, and a professional book, *Teaching Middle School Writers: What Every English Teacher Needs to Know*.

For Scholastic, Robb has completed several best sellers including the second edition of *Teaching Reading in Middle School, Differentiating Reading Instruction, Teaching Reading in Social Studies, Science, and*

Math, and her newest, *Unlocking Complex Texts*. Robb has designed classroom libraries for Scholastic for grades 3 to 9.

In addition to writing *TeamMakers: Positively Impacting the Lives of Children through District-Wide Dreaming, Collaborating, and Change*, Laura and her son Evan, a middle school principal, have teamed up to write *Schools Filled With Readers* (Benchmark Publishing).

Robb is a keynote and featured speaker at conferences and leads workshops all over the country and in Canada. She writes articles for education journals. She is a regular contributor to www.therobbreviewblog.com and has a series of podcasts with Evan Robb that you can access on therobbreviewpodcast.podbean.com

WHAT EDUCATORS ARE SAYING ABOUT LAURA ROBB

"The day whizzed by because Laura's passion for reading and writing motivated us to do everything she wanted us to bring to our students: read, write, discuss, analyze, and collaborate."

"You can tell Robb still teaches because what we learned was practical and doable."

"By her having us work in collaborative groups, I understood the benefits of having students learn in teams. Robb has a way of honoring us where we are, giving us the courage to take risks, and try what we are doing with our students."

"Her keynote on Teaching Reading and Writing To Prepare Students for Their Future made us laugh and also offered excellent ideas that showed everyone the changes in teaching and learning practices needed to make this happen."

"I wish the two-hour session could have been all day. Learned so much about using an anchor text to teach reading. Engaged every minute!"

KEYNOTES

All keynotes listed below can be adjusted to meet the needs of your school event or conference.

TEAMMAKERS

Invite Laura and Evan to explain why making star pudding empowers central office staff, school administrators, and teachers to collaborate and communicate their educational hopes and dreams. When these stakeholders work as a team and deepen their understanding of each other's stories, they tap into their creative thinking, talent, and innovative ideas to bring about positive changes throughout a district. To develop this culture of courage and respect for diverse ideas, Laura and Evan will offer specific suggestions for getting started and moving forward.

CREATING A CULTURE OF READING

Laura and Evan team up to show you what the principal and literacy coach can do to create a building-wide culture of reading. By viewing photographs of middle school students, listening to stories and practical tips, you'll understand how your school can cultivate a desire to read among all students.

ENGAGEMENT, MOTIVATION, & MEANINGFUL LEARNING

In this keynote, Laura will define and refine the terms engagement and motivation by using stories, students' work, and self-evaluations. She will offer practical ways to engage students at different reading and writing levels.

DIFFERENTIATING READING INSTRUCTION

Laura discusses why differentiating reading instruction can improve the reading skill and achievement of all learners. Along with practical tips for finding materials and supporting a class of diverse readers, Laura will also share the importance of writing about reading, opportunities for discussing books, and having choices and 20-minutes of independent reading a day.

FULL DAY ACTIVE-LEARNING WORKSHOPS

At these workshops, teachers learn in collaborative groups and practice reading and writing strategies and skills they can immediately bring back to their students. Schools can request Robb to design a literacy workshop or series of workshops that meet their specific needs.

MULTIPLE TEXTS MOTIVATE, ENGAGE, AND REACH ALL READERS, GRADES 4-8

This workshops open with how to choose an anchor text and organize it for instruction. Anchor text lessons are interactive and become the common text that allows you to think aloud and model how you respond and apply strategies. Multiple texts allow teachers to differentiate reading instruction. That's why groups will read different texts of the same genre and theme, create discussions questions, engage in literary discussions, and write about their reading in notebooks. Robb will also discuss assessment.

STUDENT-LED LITERARY CONVERSATIONS, GRADES 5 TO 9

When students create their own discussion questions and lead literary conversations, engagement and motivation to read and share ideas soar! In this workshop, you'll practice composing high level questions, essential questions, as well as review using literary elements and texts features and structures to move deeply into texts' meanings. We'll start with whole-class, teacher-led discussions and move to student-led partner and small group discussions. You'll use prompts that keep a discussion moving forward and experience the benefits of actively listening and responding to what others say. There will be forms to help you and students evaluate participation, and you'll review other kinds of assessments.

TEAMMAKERS WORKSHOP FOR CENTRAL OFFICE STAFF, PRINCIPALS, LIBRARIANS, AND TEACHER REPRESENTATIVES FROM EACH SCHOOL.

Laura and Evan will work with the entire group and small groups.

First, the entire team will identify division-wide challenges. Then, Laura and Evan will divide the group into teams who will prioritize challenges and then discuss ways to address them. Groups record their thinking on chart paper that will be shared with everyone. Next, teams study the various charts and list their top three priorities and agree on the three to address. After organizing three groups, members will build on their discussion notes to develop a plan. Each team will address one challenge by first identifying specific elements and then adding their ideas. The workshop closes with groups sharing their plans, adjusting and refining ideas based on feedback, and having a document they can share with all stakeholders. Laura and Evan will also suggest next steps.

TWO-HOUR FEATURED WORKSHOPS

Ideal for conferences, these sessions are for grades 4 on up and can be one to two hours.

VOCABULARY IS COMPREHENSION, FOR GRADES 1 TO 5

In this session, participants will practice a wide range of vocabulary strategies, always in the context of texts students are reading. Participants will use texts in different genres and experience why it's important to teach words in sets and how this enlarges students' word knowledge.

INTRODUCING UNITS OF STUDY THAT ENGAGE & MOTIVATE STUDENTS

Robb will model how a short folktale and having several poems for students to choose from can build excitement for a unit of study. In addition to partner discussions, participants will write in their notebooks. Robb will also demonstrate how a slower entry into a unit let teachers know who's ready to move on and who needs reteaching.

STUDENT-LED SMALL GROUP DISCUSSIONS

Participants will use the Fishbowl Technique as a way to show students what a productive student-led discussion looks like and how it works. Next, they will form small groups and practice student-led discussions using a short text and prompts to keep the discussion moving forward. Discussions can focus on questions participants compose or applying literary elements to texts.

TEACHING READING USING AN ANCHOR TEXT

In this workshop, participants will study in depth the benefits of teaching reading with an anchor text. Robb will provide a planning guide for anchor text lessons, model with a text, and then invite teachers to practice planning and implementing an anchor text lesson with a partner.

HOW TO CONNECT WITH LAURA ROBB

Email: laurarobb@comcast.net
Website: lrobb.com
Twitter: @LRobbTeacher

EVAN ROBB

Evan Robb is a principal, author, blogger, and a sought-after speaker. He has over twenty years of experience serving as a building-level principal. Evan leads sustainable change initiatives that transform school culture, increase achievement, and prepare students for their future.

His first book titled, *The Principal's Leadership Sourcebook: Free Up Your Time to Focus on Leadership* was published by Scholastic in the fall of 2007. Evan and Laura Robb are excited to collaborate with Dave and Shelly Burgess for their newest book, *TeamMakers*.

Evan encourages you to explore The Robb Review Blog and Scholastic EDU for more of his thoughts on teaching, learning, and leadership. All of Evan's writing focuses on looking ahead, not looking back. In addition, Evan also has a podcast, The Robb Review Podcast. He is honored to be named one of the top 25 educational leaders to follow on Twitter.

Evan offers inspirational keynotes, workshops, and ongoing professional learning opportunities across the country on leadership, mindset, culture, impactful change, and how to improve literacy in schools. Evan has shared his ideas with thousands of educators at dozens of workshops across the country.

WHAT PEOPLE ARE SAYING ABOUT EVAN ROBB AND LAURA ROBB

"Evan integrates story, humor, and at times deep emotions allowing me to make a personal connection to his message."

"It is very clear to me: Evan and Laura love sharing their stories and passion for leadership and education."

"I think this is the first mother-son keynote I have ever heard, and all I can say is I want to hear it again! Great job!"

"I have followed Evan for a few years on social media. He shares great ideas on education and leadership. Hearing Evan takes the experience to a whole new level. Evan, I am a fan!"

"Evan is polished and professional. For a well known educator, he is amazingly friendly and down to earth. He is one of us!"

KEYNOTES

All keynotes listed below can be adjusted to meet the needs of your school event or conference.

TEAMMAKERS: POSITIVELY IMPACTING THE LIVES OF CHILDREN THROUGH DISTRICT-WIDE DREAMING, PLANNING, AND COLLABORATING

Invite Laura and Evan to explain why making star pudding empowers central office staff, school administrators, and teachers to collaborate and communicate their educational hopes and dreams. When these stakeholders work as a team and deepen their understanding of each other's stories, they tap into their creative thinking, talent, and innovative ideas to bring about positive changes throughout a district. To develop this culture of courage and respect for diverse ideas, Laura and Evan will offer specific suggestions for getting started and moving forward.

CREATING A CULTURE OF READING

Laura and Evan team up to show you what the principal and literacy coach can do to create a building-wide culture of reading. By viewing photographs of middle school students, listening to stories and practical tips, you'll understand how your school can cultivate a desire to read among all students.

DISRUPTING YOUR ROUTINE AND FINDING YOUR GREATNESS

In this keynote, through story and images, Evan will share his thinking on the impact of mindset on personal and professional growth. Disrupting your routine and letting go of what's holding you back and how you view change impacts your decisions, choices, and success. Evan will challenge the status quo and challenge your staff to reflect on their work patterns and the changes they can make to get new and better results.

CULTURE, CLIMATE, AND LEADERSHIP

In this keynote, Evan, through story and personal experience, shares the importance of establishing a positive school culture and climate. Learn eight specific strategies you can start right away to lead change to create an environment staff want to work in and a school students want to attend.

A FULL DAY ACTIVE-LEARNING WORKSHOP

Laura and Evan will work with the entire group and small groups. First, the entire team will identify division-wide challenges. Then, Laura and Evan will divide the group into teams who will prioritize challenges and then discuss ways to address them. Groups record their thinking on chart paper that will be shared with everyone. Next, teams study the various charts and list their top three priorities and agree on the three to address. After organizing three groups, members will build on their discussion notes to develop a plan. Each team will address one challenge by first identifying specific elements and then adding their ideas. The workshop closes with groups sharing their plans, adjusting and refining ideas based on feedback, and having a document they can share with all stakeholders. Laura and Evan will also suggest next steps.

WORKSHOPS

Each workshop can be one or two hours and are ideal for grades K–12.

MINDSET MATTERS

Staff will see how mindset, disrupting routines, and letting go of what is holding us back can lead to innovations in teaching. Evan will share stories, pose questions, and offer suggestions on how the choices we make can change the trajectories of adults and children.

THINK LIKE AN ENTREPRENEUR: MARKET YOUR SCHOOL

Evan pulls upon his MBA skills to share 10 specific strategies you can use to harness technologies and social media to define your school's brand and to promote your brand to your community, staff, and students.

YOU CAN'T FIRE YOUR WAY TO EXCELLENCE

In this workshop, Evan shares 5 specific strategies he has learned to improve staff performance. Effective principals understand it takes time for a teacher to grow and develop the skills necessary to integrate best practices into a learner-centered environment. Effective principals understand that at times, a variety of supports can improve teachers' practice and class management. It's important to understand this: a principal cannot build a positive student-focused culture by removing staff in hopes of the perfect teacher showing up for an interview.

TIME TO LET GO!

This workshop is a combination of humor, nostalgia, and change. Evan takes your staff on a journey and highlights 7 traditions that many hold near and dear but need to go. Learn how to challenge some of these traditions and strategies to bring about effective change for staff and students.

HOW TO CONNECT WITH EVAN ROBB

Email: evanrobb@comcast.net
Website: van-robb.com | robbcommunications.com
Facebook: The Robb Review
Twitter: @ERobbPrincipal

MORE FROM

DAVE BURGESS Consulting, Inc.

Since 2012, DBCI has been publishing books that inspire and equip educators to be their best. For more information on our DBCI titles or to purchase bulk orders for your school, district, or book study, visit DaveBurgessconsulting.com/DBCIbooks.

MORE FROM THE LIKE A PIRATE™ SERIES

- *Teach Like a PIRATE* by Dave Burgess
- *eXPlore Like a Pirate* by Michael Matera
- *Learn Like a Pirate* by Paul Solarz
- *Play Like a Pirate* by Quinn Rollins
- *Run Like a Pirate* by Adam Welcome

LEAD LIKE A PIRATE™ SERIES

- *Lead Like a PIRATE* by Shelley Burgess and Beth Houf
- *Balance Like a Pirate* by Jessica Cabeen, Jessica Johnson, and Sarah Johnson
- *Lead beyond Your Title* by Nili Bartley
- *Lead with Culture* by Jay Billy
- *Lead with Literacy* by Mandy Ellis

LEADERSHIP & SCHOOL CULTURE

- *Culturize* by Jimmy Casas
- *Escaping the School Leader's Dunk Tank* by Rebecca Coda and Rick Jetter
- *From Teacher to Leader* by Starr Sackstein
- *The Innovator's Mindset* by George Couros
- *Kids Deserve It!* by Todd Nesloney and Adam Welcome
- *Let Them Speak* by Rebecca Coda and Rick Jetter
- *The Limitless School* by Abe Hege and Adam Dovico
- *The Pepper Effect* by Sean Gaillard
- *The Principled Principal* by Jeffrey Zoul and Anthony McConnell
- *Relentless* by Hamish Brewer
- *The Secret Solution* by Todd Whitaker, Sam Miller, and Ryan Donlan
- *Start. Right. Now.* by Todd Whitaker, Jeffrey Zoul, and Jimmy Casas
- *Stop. Right. Now.* by Jimmy Casas and Jeffrey Zoul
- *Unmapped Potential* by Julie Hasson and Missy Lennard
- *They Call Me "Mr. De"* by Frank DeAngelis
- *Your School Rocks* by Ryan McLane and Eric Lowe

TECHNOLOGY & TOOLS

- *50 Things You Can Do with Google Classroom* by Alice Keeler and Libbi Miller
- *50 Things to Go Further with Google Classroom* by Alice Keeler and Libbi Miller
- *140 Twitter Tips for Educators* by Brad Currie, Billy Krakower, and Scott Rocco
- *Block Breaker* by Brian Aspinall
- *Code Breaker* by Brian Aspinall
- *Google Apps for Littles* by Christine Pinto and Alice Keeler
- *Master the Media* by Julie Smith
- *Shake Up Learning* by Kasey Bell
- *Social LEADia* by Jennifer Casa-Todd
- *Teaching Math with Google Apps* by Alice Keeler and Diana Herrington
- *Teachingland* by Amanda Fox and Mary Ellen Weeks

TEACHING METHODS & MATERIALS

- *All 4s and 5s* by Andrew Sharos
- *The Classroom Chef* by John Stevens and Matt Vaudrey
- *Ditch That Homework* by Matt Miller and Alice Keeler
- *Ditch That Textbook* by Matt Miller
- *Don't Ditch That Tech* by Matt Miller, Nate Ridgway, and Angelia Ridgway
- *EDrenaline Rush* by John Meehan
- *Educated by Design* by Michael Cohen, The Tech Rabbi
- *The EduProtocol Field Guide* by Marlena Hebern and Jon Corippo
- *Instant Relevance* by Denis Sheeran
- *LAUNCH* by John Spencer and A.J. Juliani
- *Make Learning MAGICAL* by Tisha Richmond
- *Pure Genius* by Don Wettrick
- *The Revolution* by Darren Ellwein and Derek McCoy
- *Shift This!* by Joy Kirr
- *Spark Learning* by Ramsey Musallam
- *Sparks in the Dark* by Travis Crowder and Todd Nesloney
- *Table Talk Math* by John Stevens
- *The Wild Card* by Hope and Wade King
- *The Writing on the Classroom Wall* by Steve Wyborney

INSPIRATION, PROFESSIONAL GROWTH & PERSONAL DEVELOPMENT

- *Be REAL* by Tara Martin
- *Be the One for Kids* by Ryan Sheehy
- Creatively Productive by Lisa Johnson
- *The EduNinja Mindset* by Jennifer Burdis
- *Empower Our Girls* by Lynmara Colón and Adam Welcome
- *The Four O'Clock Faculty* by Rich Czyz
- *How Much Water Do We Have?* by Pete and Kris Nunweiler
- *P Is for Pirate* by Dave and Shelley Burgess
- *A Passion for Kindness* by Tamara Letter
- *The Path to Serendipity* by Allyson Apsey
- *Sanctuaries* by Dan Tricarico
- *Shattering the Perfect Teacher Myth* by Aaron Hogan

- *Stories from Webb* by Todd Nesloney
- *Talk to Me* by Kim Bearden
- *The Zen Teacher* by Dan Tricarico
- *Through the Lens of Serendipity* by Allyson Apsey

CHILDREN'S BOOKS

- *Dolphins in Trees* by Aaron Polansky
- *The Princes of Serendip* by Allyson Apsey
- *I Want to Be a Lot* by Ashley Savage
- *Zom-Be a Design Thinker* by Amanda Fox